Scott Foresman

Reading

Grade 5

Spelling Workbook

Scott Foresman

Editorial Offices: Glenview, Illinois • Parsippany, New Jersey • New York, New York
Sales Offices: Reading, Massachusetts • Duluth, Georgia • Glenview, Illinois
Carrollton, Texas • Ontario, California

Editorial Offices
Glenview, Illinois • Parsippany, New Jersey • New York, New York

Sales Offices
Reading, Massachusetts • Duluth, Georgia • Glenview, Illinois
Carrollton, Texas • Ontario, California

ISBN 0-328-01653-5

3 4 5 6 7 8 9 10-PRO-06 05 04 03 02 01

Table of Contents

Unit 1

	Pretest	Think and Practice	Proofread and Write	Review
Relating to Others				
From the Diary of Leigh Botts Vowels Sounds with *r*	1	2	3	4
Faith and Eddie Short *e* and Long *e*	5	6	7	8
Looking for a Home Vowel Sounds in *boy* and *out*	9	10	11	12
Meeting Mr. Henry Long Vowels *a, i, o*	13	14	15	16
Eloise Greenfield Vowel Sounds in *rule, use, off*	17	18	19	20

Unit 2

	Pretest	Think and Practice	Proofread and Write	Review
My World and Yours				
The Diver and the Dolphins Consonant Sounds /j/ and /k/	21	22	23	24
The Fury of a Hurricane Words with *kn, mb, gh, st*	25	26	27	28
Dwaina Brooks Compound Words I	29	30	31	32
Everglades Short Vowels *a, i, o,* and *u*	33	34	35	36
Missing Links Prefixes *dis-, un-, mid-,* and *pre-*	37	38	39	40

Unit 3

A Job Well Done	Pretest	Think and Practice	Proofread and Write	Review
Going with the Flow Adding -s and -es	41	42	43	44
Kate Shelley: Bound for Legend Irregular Plurals	45	46	47	48
The Marble Champ Contractions	49	50	51	52
From Bees to Honey Capitalization	53	54	55	56
Babe to the Rescue Possessives	57	58	59	60

Unit 4

Time and Time Again	Pretest	Think and Practice	Proofread and Write	Review
The Yangs' First Thanksgiving Homophones	61	62	63	64
The Jr. Iditarod Race Including All the Letters	65	66	67	68
The Night Alone Adding -ed and -ing, -er, and -est	69	70	71	72
The Heart of a Runner Vowels with No Sound Clues	73	74	75	76
The Memory Box Vowels in Final Syllables	77	78	79	80

Unit 5

	Pretest	Think and Practice	Proofread and Write	Review
Traveling On				
I Want to Vote! Words with *ng, nk, th*	81	82	83	84
The Long Path to Freedom Suffixes *-able, -ible, -ant, -ent*	85	86	87	88
from **Chester Cricket's Pigeon Ride** Suffixes *-ous, -ion, -ation*	89	90	91	92
Passage to Freedom: The Sugihara Story Compound Words 2	93	94	95	96
Paul Revere's Ride Related Words	97	98	99	100

Unit 6

	Pretest	Think and Practice	Proofread and Write	Review
Think of It!				
The Baker's Neighbor Easily Confused Words	101	102	103	104
Andy's Secret Ingredient Using Just Enough Letters	105	106	107	108
In the Days of King Adobe More Vowels with *r*	109	110	111	112
Just Telling the Truth Getting Letters in Correct Order	113	114	115	116
Is It Real? Related Words	117	118	119	120

Spelling: Vowel Sounds with *r*

Pretest Directions: Fold back the page along the dotted line. On the blanks, write the spelling words as they are dictated. When you have finished the test, unfold the page and check your words.

1._____	**1.** His brother joined the **army**.
2._____	**2.** We must eat or **starve**.
3._____	**3.** The cut left a small **scar**.
4._____	**4.** The **garbage** can is full.
5._____	**5.** I do not want to **argue**.
6._____	**6.** Their **apartment** was large.
7._____	**7.** Jess plays songs on her **guitar**.
8._____	**8.** King River is in **Arkansas**.
9._____	**9.** Thea eats well-done **hamburger**.
10._____	**10.** **Return** your library books.
11._____	**11.** He did it on **purpose**.
12._____	**12.** The **surface** of the water is clear.
13._____	**13.** A cat will **curl** up to sleep.
14._____	**14.** What is in the woman's **purse**?
15._____	**15.** The **furniture** was very old.
16._____	**16.** A lion tamer has **courage**.
17._____	**17.** I write in my **journal** every day.
18._____	**18.** Show **courtesy** toward others.
19._____	**19.** I **nourish** myself with good food.
20._____	**20.** Lylia is going on a long **journey**.

Notes for Home: Your child took a pretest on words that have vowel sounds with the letter *r*. *Home Activity:* Help your child learn misspelled words before the final test. Your child should look at the word, say it, spell it aloud, and then spell it with eyes shut.

Think and Practice

Spelling: Vowel Sounds with *r*

Word List

army	apartment	purpose	courage
starve	guitar	surface	journal
scar	Arkansas	curl	courtesy
garbage	hamburger	purse	nourish
argue	return	furniture	journey

Directions: Choose the words from the box that have the vowel sound with **r** that you hear in **hurt**. Write each word in the correct column.

Vowel-r sound spelled ur

1. _____
2. _____
3. _____
4. _____
5. _____
6. _____
7. _____

Vowel-r sound spelled our

8. _____
9. _____
10. _____
11. _____
12. _____

Directions: Decide where to add the letters **ar** in each letter group to spell a word from the box. Write the word on the line.

13. guit _____
14. sc _____
15. my _____
16. kansas _____
17. stve _____
18. gue _____
19. gbage _____
20. aptment _____

Notes for Home: Your child spelled words where the letter *r* changes the vowel sound. *Home Activity:* Read a magazine article with your child. Together, see how many words you can find that have the same vowel sounds and spellings as *scar, curl,* and *journal.*

2   Spelling: Vowel Sounds with *r*

Name _____

Spelling: Vowel Sounds with *r*

Directions: Proofread this journal entry. Find five spelling mistakes. Use the proofreading marks to correct each mistake.

June 13—I have been writing in my

jurnal since March. Since then I

have been working on our apertment.

First, I rearranged the furniture.

Then I painted. I had to aregue with

Dad about painting the serface of

the kitchen counter. It took courage

to paint it purple! Now, though, I've

decided to retern to the original

color, and both Dad and I are happy.

Maybe I'll even put the furniture back.

≣	Make a capital.
⁄	Make a small letter.
∧	Add something.
ꝰ	Take out something.
⊙	Add a period.
¶	Begin a new paragraph.

Spelling Tip
return

How can you remember that **return** has a **u** in the middle? Think of this hint: Make a "U" **turn** to re**turn**. Check the journal entry to see if this word is spelled correctly.

Word List

army	purpose
starve	surface
scar	curl
garbage	purse
argue	furniture
apartment	courage
guitar	journal
Arkansas	courtesy
hamburger	nourish
return	journey

Write a Journal Entry

Imagine you have a problem you need to solve. On a separate sheet of paper, write a journal entry that describes your problem plus an idea for solving it. Try to use at least five of your spelling words.

Notes for Home: Your child spelled words where the letter *r* changes the vowel sound, such as in *scar, curl,* and *journal.* **Home Activity:** Write each spelling word with the letters scrambled. See if your child can unscramble each word and spell it correctly.

© Scott Foresman 5

Proofread and Write

Spelling: Vowel Sounds with *r*

Word List

army	argue	hamburger	curl	journal
starve	apartment	return	purse	courtesy
scar	guitar	purpose	furniture	nourish
garbage	Arkansas	surface	courage	journey

Directions: Choose the word from the box that best completes each statement. Write the word on the line to the left. Look at the pairs of words that are being compared. See the example below.

Crawl is to baby as walk is to adult.

_____ **1.** *City* is to *Little Rock* as *state* is to _____.

_____ **2.** *Blow* is to *horn* as *strum* is to _____.

_____ **3.** *Sailors* are to *navy* as *soldiers* are to _____.

_____ **4.** *Groceries* are to *food* as *trash* is to _____.

_____ **5.** *Car* is to *bicycle* as *palace* is to _____.

_____ **6.** *Friends* are to *agree* as *enemies* are to _____.

_____ **7.** *Metal* is to *scratch* as *skin* is to _____.

_____ **8.** *Air* is to *suffocate* as *food* is to _____.

_____ **9.** *Pig* is to *sausage* as *cow* is to _____.

_____ **10.** *Laundry* is to *basket* as *money* is to _____.

_____ **11.** *Coat* is to *clothing* as *table* is to _____.

_____ **12.** *Coward* is to *fear* as *hero* is to _____.

_____ **13.** *Begin* is to *finish* as *leave* is to _____.

_____ **14.** *Intentionally* is to *intention* as *purposely* is to _____.

Directions: Choose the word from the box that has the same or nearly the same meaning as the word or words below. Write the word on the line.

15. politeness _____

16. feed _____

17. trip _____

18. daily record _____

19. roll up _____

20. face or side _____

Notes for Home: Your child spelled words in which the letter *r* changes the vowel sound. *Home Activity:* Look around the room with your child. Together, see how many items you can find whose names have the same vowel sounds and spellings as in *scar, curl,* and *journal.*

Spelling: Short e and Long e

Pretest Directions: Fold back the page along the dotted line. On the blanks, write the spelling words as they are dictated. When you have finished the test, unfold the page and check your words.

1._____

2._____

3._____

4._____

5._____

6._____

7._____

8._____

9._____

10._____

11._____

12._____

13._____

14._____

15._____

16._____

17._____

18._____

19._____

20._____

1. The weight is **heavy**.

2. Let's plan **ahead**.

3. **Measure** the triangle.

4. The bus **already** came.

5. She is not **jealous** of others.

6. Flowers grow in the **meadow**.

7. The soldier held his **weapon**.

8. Did you hear what I **said**?

9. Let's play **again**.

10. Lean **against** the wall.

11. Juan earned a college **degree**.

12. Say **cheese** for the camera!

13. Sara is determined to **succeed**.

14. The principal gave a **speech**.

15. The **breeze** cooled us off.

16. Our **goalie** blocked the point.

17. Please, cut a **piece** of pizza.

18. I **believe** it is true.

19. The **thief** took it.

20. Hail to the **chief**.

Notes for Home: Your child took a pretest on words that have the short *e* and long *e* sounds. *Home Activity:* Help your child learn misspelled words before the final test. Your child can underline the word parts that caused the problems and concentrate on those parts.

Think and Practice

Spelling: Short e and Long e

Word List			
heavy	meadow	degree	goalie
ahead	weapon	cheese	piece
measure	said	succeed	believe
already	again	speech	thief
jealous	against	breeze	chief

Directions: Choose the words from the box that have the **long e** sound. Write each word in the correct column.

Long e spelled ee

1. _____
2. _____
3. _____
4. _____
5. _____

Long e spelled ie

6. _____
7. _____
8. _____
9. _____
10. _____

Directions: Write the **short e** word from the box that begins and ends with the same letters as each word below.

11. mellow _____
12. accident _____
13. hay _____
14. action _____
15. spend _____

16. jobs _____
17. accepted _____
18. anybody _____
19. woman _____
20. mile _____

HEAVY CHEESE

Notes for Home: Your child spelled words with the short e sound spelled *ea* and *ai (ahead, said)* and the long e sound spelled *ee* and *ie (cheese, piece)*. **Home Activity:** Read a brief newspaper article with your child. Together, find all the short e and long e words you can.

Spelling: Short e and Long e

Directions: Proofread this description. Find five spelling mistakes. Use the proofreading marks to correct each mistake.

> What are my best friends like? For one thing, they are never jelous of me. They like to see me succead and to get ahead. My best friends would never turn agianst me. Also, they trust me and always beleeve what I have said to them. They don't mind if I give them a peace of advice. If you have friends like that, you are already a very lucky person indeed!

≡	Make a capital.
/	Make a small letter.
∧	Add something.
⌐	Take out something.
⊙	Add a period.
¶	Begin a new paragraph.

Spelling Tip
piece
Don't confuse the word **piece** with **peace**. Remember this hint: I want a **pie**ce of **pie**.

Word List
heavy
ahead
measure
already
jealous
meadow
weapon
said
again
against
degree
cheese
succeed
speech
breeze
goalie
piece
believe
thief
chief

Write a Description

Think about a good friend. How does your friend act? What does your friend look like? What sorts of activities do you both enjoy? What makes this person a good friend? On a separate sheet of paper, write a description of your friend. Try to use at least five of your spelling words.

Notes for Home: Your child spelled words with the short *e* sound spelled *ea* and *ai* (ah*ea*d, s*ai*d) and the long *e* sound spelled *ee* and *ie* (ch*ee*se, p*ie*ce). **Home Activity:** Together, look at pictures in a magazine to find items whose names have the short *e* and long *e* sounds.

Spelling: Short e and Long e

Word List

heavy	meadow	degree	goalie
ahead	weapon	cheese	piece
measure	said	succeed	believe
already	again	speech	thief
jealous	against	breeze	chief

Directions: Choose the word from the box that best matches each clue. Write the letters of the word on the blanks. The boxed letters tell what you'll find in each word.

1. think to be true
2. a position on the soccer team
3. one more time
4. a college title
5. a gun, for example
6. a cool wind
7. spoke
8. a formal talk
9. a grassy field
10. use a ruler
11. opposed to
12. a dairy product

1. __ __ ☐ __ __ __ __
2. __ __ ☐ __ __ __
3. __ __ __ ☐ __ __
4. __ __ __ __ ☐ __ __
5. __ __ __ __ ☐ __
6. __ ☐ __ __ __ __
7. __ ☐ __ __ __
8. __ __ __ __ ☐ __
9. __ __ __ __ ☐ __
10. __ __ __ __ __ ☐ __
11. __ __ __ __ __ ☐ __
12. __ __ __ __ ☐ __

What you'll find in each word: _____

Directions: Choose the word from the box that is most opposite in meaning for each word or words below. Write the word on the line.

13. light _____
14. fail _____
15. whole _____
16. behind _____

17. not yet _____
18. donor _____
19. follower _____
20. content _____

Notes for Home: Your child spelled words with the short *e* sound spelled *ea* and *ai (ahead, said)* and the long *e* sound spelled *ee* and *ie (cheese, piece)*. **Home Activity:** Have your child spell each spelling word and tell whether it has a short *e* or long *e* sound.

Spelling: Vowel Sounds in *boy* and *out*

Pretest Directions: Fold back the page along the dotted line. On the blanks, write the spelling words as they are dictated. When you have finished the test, unfold the page and check your words.

1._____

2._____

3._____

4._____

5._____

6._____

7._____

8._____

9._____

10._____

11._____

12._____

13._____

14._____

15._____

16._____

17._____

18._____

19._____

20._____

1. You have to make a **choice**.

2. Drums can be very **noisy**.

3. Old fruit will **spoil**.

4. On the bottle it said **poison**.

5. Chicago is a big city in **Illinois**.

6. Good friends are always **loyal**.

7. Rain will **destroy** the drawing.

8. Wasps **annoy** me.

9. The **oyster** made a pearl.

10. He went on a long **voyage**.

11. The recipe needs baking **powder**.

12. Bring your **towel** to the pool.

13. I like to shop **downtown**.

14. You must swim or **drown**.

15. The dog will **growl**.

16. They paid the wrong **amount**.

17. This is **our** house.

18. Let's play **outside**.

19. Please sit on the **couch**.

20. Ants **surround** the ice cream.

Notes for Home: Your child took a pretest on words that have the vowel sounds heard in *boy* and *out*. **Home Activity:** Help your child learn misspelled words before the final test. Dictate the word and have your child spell the word aloud for you or write it on paper.

Think and Practice

Spelling: Vowel Sounds in *boy* and *out*

Word List			
choice	loyal	powder	amount
noisy	destroy	towel	our
spoil	annoy	downtown	outside
poison	oyster	drown	couch
Illinois	voyage	growl	surround

Directions: Choose the words from the box that have the vowel sound in **boy**.
Write each word in the correct column.

Vowel sound spelled oy

1. _____
2. _____
3. _____
4. _____
5. _____

Vowel sound spelled oi

6. _____
7. _____
8. _____
9. _____
10. _____

Directions: Write the word from the box that belongs in each group of words. Hint: The word will have the vowel sound in **out**.

11. inside, between, _____

12. oink, moo, _____

13. chair, table, _____

14. uptown, midtown, _____

15. napkin, cloth, _____

16. circle, enclose, _____

17. liquid, paste, _____

18. swim, sink, _____

19. your, their, _____

20. cost, price, _____

Notes for Home: Your child spelled words that have the vowel sounds heard in *boy* spelled *oi* and *oy* and *out* spelled *ow* and *ou*. **Home Activity:** Together, write the spelling words on slips of paper. Take turns choosing words and saying them aloud for the other person to spell.

© Scott Foresman 5

Name _____

Spelling: Vowel Sounds in *boy* and *out*

Directions: Proofread this letter. Find five spelling mistakes. Use the proofreading marks to correct each mistake.

☰	Make a capital.
╱	Make a small letter.
∧	Add something.
⌿	Take out something.
⊙	Add a period.
⁋	Begin a new paragraph.

Dear Advice Giver,

   Owr family lives in Illinoy. We just moved to a new home dountown. I should be glad, but it's starting to annoy me. It always seems very noisy outside. Strangers surrownd me. I'm afraid this move will destroy my life. Tell me what to do. Do I have another choyce?

Sincerely,

Stuck in Downtown

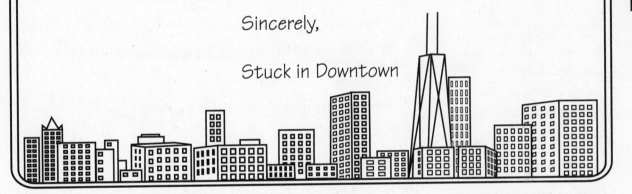

Word List

choice	loyal	powder	amount
noisy	destroy	towel	our
spoil	annoy	downtown	outside
poison	oyster	drown	couch
Illinois	voyage	growl	surround

Spelling Tip
Illinois
Don't forget the final **-s** in **Illinois.** Always remember to add the final **-s,** even though the final **-s** is silent.

Write a Reply

Imagine you are the "Advice Giver" who received the letter above. On a separate sheet of paper, write a reply that tells "Stuck in Downtown" what to do. Try to use at least five of your spelling words.

Notes for Home: Your child spelled words with the vowel sounds heard in *boy* spelled *oi* and *oy* and *out* spelled *ow* and *ou*. **Home Activity:** Spell each spelling word slowly, one letter at a time. When your child knows the word, have him or her complete its spelling.

Name _____

Spelling: Vowel Sounds in *boy* and *out*

REVIEW

Word List			
choice	loyal	powder	amount
noisy	destroy	towel	our
spoil	annoy	downtown	outside
poison	oyster	drown	couch
Illinois	voyage	growl	surround

Directions: Choose the word from the box that best answers each question. Write the word on the line.

_____ 1. What state is west of Indiana?

_____ 2. What do you call a trip across the ocean?

_____ 3. What piece of furniture can you relax on?

_____ 4. What is very dangerous if swallowed?

_____ 5. What do you use to dry off after a shower?

_____ 6. What place is the opposite of *uptown?*

_____ 7. What sea creature has a pearl in its shell?

_____ 8. What is the opposite of *inside?*

_____ 9. What is soft, dry, and dusty?

_____ 10. What sound does a hungry stomach make?

Directions: Choose the word from the box that has the same or nearly the same meaning as each word or words below. Write the word on the line.

11. loud _____

12. enclose _____

13. selection _____

14. sink _____

15. bother _____

16. owned together _____

17. ruin _____

18. decay _____

19. sum _____

20. faithful _____

Notes for Home: Your child spelled words that have the vowel sounds heard in *boy* spelled *oi* and *oy (choice, loyal)* and *out* spelled *ow* and *ou (towel, couch)*. **Home Activity:** Read a short story with your child. Look for words that have the vowel sounds heard in *boy* and *out*.

Spelling: Long Vowels *a, i, o*

Pretest Directions: Fold back the page along the dotted line. On the blanks, write the spelling words as they are dictated. When you have finished the test, unfold the page and check your words.

1._____	1. Use your **brain** to think.
2._____	2. I draw on **plain** paper.
3._____	3. What seat did you **claim**?
4._____	4. Don't **complain**, just fix it.
5._____	5. Spring is my **favorite** season.
6._____	6. Fact can be **stranger** than fiction.
7._____	7. The **aliens** went home.
8._____	8. I want to go on a **vacation**.
9._____	9. We ran on the **sidewalk**.
10._____	10. He slid down the **slide**.
11._____	11. You need water to **survive**.
12._____	12. Stealing is a **crime**.
13._____	13. Lin is at the **bowling** alley.
14._____	14. Who is the **owner** of this dog?
15._____	15. The **arrow** points up.
16._____	16. She threw a **snowball**.
17._____	17. Lisa ate the **whole** pie.
18._____	18. Spin the **globe**.
19._____	19. The **antelope** plays on the range.
20._____	20. The **slope** is steep.

Notes for Home: Your child took a pretest on words that have the long vowels *a, i,* and *o*. *Home Activity:* Help your child learn misspelled words before the final test. Your child can underline the word parts that caused the problems and concentrate on those parts.

Spelling: Long Vowels *a, i, o*

Think and Practice

Word List				
brain	favorite	sidewalk	bowling	whole
plain	stranger	slide	owner	globe
claim	aliens	survive	arrow	antelope
complain	vacation	crime	snowball	slope

Directions: Choose the words from the box that have the **long a** sound. Write each word in the correct column.

Long a spelled ai

1. _____

2. _____

3. _____

4. _____

Long a spelled a

5. _____

6. _____

7. _____

8. _____

Directions: Choose the word from the box that rhymes with the underlined word or words and completes the sentence. Write the word on the line to the left.

_____ 9. I certainly <u>hope</u> you don't fall down a _____.

_____ 10. If I were you, <u>I'd walk</u> on the _____.

_____ 11. A gift's <u>donor</u> is usually its _____.

_____ 12. You do some <u>strolling</u> in a game of _____.

_____ 13. There is <u>no ball</u> that stings like a _____.

_____ 14. Will you eat a <u>roll</u>, either half or _____?

_____ 15. It's fun to <u>ride</u> on a slippery _____.

_____ 16. If it's sharp and <u>narrow</u>, it might be an _____.

_____ 17. "Sorry, you <u>can't elope</u>," said the papa _____.

_____ 18. It's never a good <u>time</u> to commit a _____.

_____ 19. I bought a long <u>robe</u> and a brand-new _____.

_____ 20. If you're still <u>alive</u>, you've managed to _____.

Notes for Home: Your child spelled words that have the long *a, i,* or *o* sound (*brain, stranger, slide, arrow, slope*). **Home Activity:** Together with your child, name other words that have the long *a, i,* or *o* sound. See how many of these words your child can spell correctly.

Spelling: Long Vowels *a, i, o*

Directions: Proofread this letter. Find five spelling mistakes. Use the proofreading marks to correct each mistake.

≡	Make a capital.
/	Make a small letter.
∧	Add something.
℘	Take out something.
⊙	Add a period.
¶	Begin a new paragraph.

Dear Aunt Esther,

On vacaition, Dad took our whoal family to our first baseball game. Now it's my favorite sport—even more than boaling! It's so cool how players slide! After the game, we met the team oner and some players on the sidewalk. I can't complain about having this much fun!

Love,

Dave

Spelling Tip

whole	owner

Remember that **long o** can be spelled with **consonant-vowel-consonant-e,** as in **whole,** but it can also be spelled with **ow,** as in **owner.** Remember which spelling to use.

Word List

brain	survive
plain	crime
claim	bowling
complain	owner
favorite	arrow
stranger	snowball
aliens	whole
vacation	globe
sidewalk	antelope
slide	slope

Write a Letter

Imagine you are Dave's Aunt Esther. On a separate sheet of paper, write a friendly letter back to Dave. Try to use at least five of your spelling words.

Notes for Home: Your child spelled words that have the long *a, i,* or *o* sounds *(brain, stranger, slide, arrow, slope)*. **Home Activity:** Say each spelling word aloud. Have your child tell whether the word has a long *a, i,* or *o* sound. Then have your child spell the word.

© Scott Foresman 5

Spelling: Long Vowels *a, i, o*

REVIEW

Word List				
brain	favorite	sidewalk	bowling	whole
plain	stranger	slide	owner	globe
claim	aliens	survive	arrow	antelope
complain	vacation	crime	snowball	slope

Directions: Choose the word from the box that best completes each sentence. Write the word on the line to the left.

_____ 1. Baseball is a popular game all over the _____.

_____ 2. It has often been called America's _____ pastime.

_____ 3. Baseball is a more popular sport than _____.

_____ 4. A _____ baseball game lasts nine innings.

_____ 5. The pitcher stands on a small _____ called a mound.

_____ 6. A good baseball pitcher can _____ an entire game.

_____ 7. In baseball, it's not a _____ to steal bases.

_____ 8. Runners _____ into bases and kick up dirt!

_____ 9. A good runner moves as swiftly as a speeding _____.

_____ 10. A good sport doesn't _____ if he or she loses.

Directions: Choose the word from the box that best matches each clue. Write the word on the line.

_____ 11. It's a very fast animal.

_____ 12. They're strangers from another planet!

_____ 13. He's new in town.

_____ 14. She's the one who bought it.

_____ 15. It's round and cold.

_____ 16. It lets you think.

_____ 17. It's not fancy.

_____ 18. It's a rest from work.

_____ 19. It's made of cement and is often found in front of houses.

_____ 20. It's something you make when you say, "I didn't do that."

Notes for Home: Your child spelled words that have the long *a, i,* or *o* sound (*brain, stranger, slide, arrow, slope*). **Home Activity:** Pick a spelling word. Give a hint about the word. (Example: *It's a long* a *word. It's in your head.*) See if your child can guess the word. (*brain*)

© Scott Foresman 5

Spelling: Vowel Sounds in *rule, use, off*

Pretest Directions: Fold back the page along the dotted line. On the blanks, write the spelling words as they are dictated. When you have finished the test, unfold the page and check your words.

1._____	**1. Choose** a shirt to wear.
2._____	2. It is time to go to **school**.
3._____	3. The **broom** is made of straw.
4._____	4. He uses a shovel to **scoop** sand.
5._____	5. There is a phone **booth** inside.
6._____	6. They **threw** away the garbage.
7._____	7. A work **crew** paved the road.
8._____	8. What a nice picture you **drew**!
9._____	9. I have found my lost **jewel**.
10._____	10. What will the **future** be like?
11._____	11. Tad likes all kinds of **music**.
12._____	12. I **usually** eat lunch outside.
13._____	13. His sense of **humor** is strange.
14._____	14. Have you ever been to **Utah**?
15._____	15. The teacher **taught** them to read.
16._____	16. It is **naughty** to be rude.
17._____	17. The couple has one **daughter**.
18._____	18. Put your **laundry** in the dryer.
19._____	19. **Sausage** is good at breakfast.
20._____	20. The ship will **launch** tomorrow.

© Scott Foresman 5

Notes for Home: Your child took a pretest on words that have vowel sounds such as those in *rule, use,* and *off.* **Home Activity:** Help your child learn misspelled words before the final test. See if there are any similar errors and discuss a memory trick that could help.

Think and Practice

Spelling: Vowel Sounds in *rule, use, off*

Word List

choose	threw	music	naughty
school	crew	usually	daughter
broom	drew	humor	laundry
scoop	jewel	Utah	sausage
booth	future	taught	launch

Directions: Choose the words from the box that have the vowel sound you hear in *off.* Write each word in the correct column.

Vowel sound spelled augh

1. _____

2. _____

3. _____

Vowel sound spelled au

4. _____

5. _____

6. _____

Directions: Complete each equation to spell a word from the box. Write the word on the line.

7. useful   –   eful   +   ually   =   _____

8. creep   –   eep   +   ew   =   _____

9. change   –   ange   +   oose   =   _____

10. Utopia   –   opia   +   ah   =   _____

11. fuel   –   el   +   ture   =   _____

12. brown   –   wn   +   om   =   _____

13. jest   –   st   +   wel   =   _____

14. scheme   –   eme   +   ool   =   _____

15. museum   –   eum   +   ic   =   _____

16. huge   –   ge   +   mor   =   _____

17. boat   –   at   +   oth   =   _____

18. scar   –   ar   +   oop   =   _____

19. thread   –   ad   +   w   =   _____

20. drive   –   ive   +   ew   =   _____

Notes for Home: Your child spelled words that have the vowel sounds heard in *rule* spelled *oo* and *ew (sch<u>oo</u>l, thr<u>ew</u>)*, *use* spelled *u (m<u>u</u>sic)*, and *off* spelled *augh* and *au (t<u>augh</u>t, l<u>au</u>ndry)*. *Home Activity:* Say each spelling word to your child. See if your child can spell it correctly.

Name_____

Spelling: Vowel Sounds in *rule, use, off*

Directions: Proofread this description. Find five spelling mistakes. Use the proofreading marks to correct each mistake.

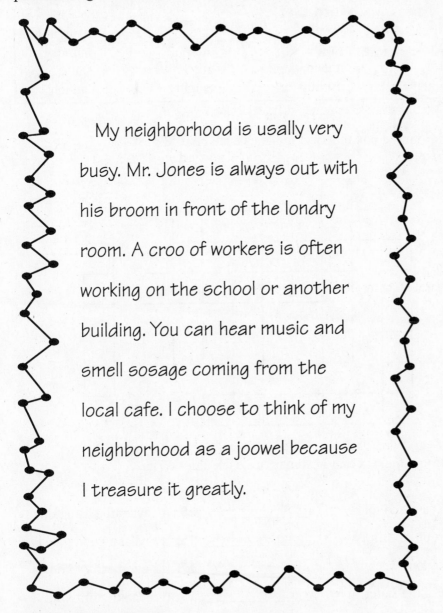

My neighborhood is usally very busy. Mr. Jones is always out with his broom in front of the londry room. A croo of workers is often working on the school or another building. You can hear music and smell sosage coming from the local cafe. I choose to think of my neighborhood as a joowel because I treasure it greatly.

≡ Make a capital.
/ Make a small letter.
∧ Add something.
ℐ Take out something.
⊙ Add a period.
¶ Begin a new paragraph.

Spelling Tip

choose

Some people forget that **choose** has two **o**'s, not one. Remember: When you **ch<u>oo</u>se,** you often pick between <u>two</u> things.

Word List

choose
school
broom
scoop
booth
threw
crew
drew
jewel
future
music
usually
humor
Utah
taught
naughty
daughter
laundry
sausage
launch

Write a Description

On a separate sheet of paper, write a description of your neighborhood or one you would like to live in. Try to use at least five of your spelling words.

Notes for Home: Your child spelled words that have the vowel sounds heard in *rule* spelled *oo* and *ew (sch<u>oo</u>l, thr<u>ew</u>),* *use* spelled *u (m<u>u</u>sic),* and *off* spelled *augh* and *au (t<u>augh</u>t, l<u>au</u>ndry).* **Home Activity:** Scramble the letters of each spelling word and have your child unscramble the words.

Proofread and Write

Spelling: Vowel Sounds in *rule, use, off*

REVIEW

Word List

choose	booth	jewel	humor	daughter
school	threw	future	Utah	laundry
broom	crew	music	taught	sausage
scoop	drew	usually	naughty	launch

Directions: Choose the word from the box that best matches each clue. Write the word in the puzzle.

Down

1. send up in the air
2. female child
4. learning place
5. small stall

Across

3. kind of meat
6. bad
7. instructed
8. dirty clothes

Directions: Choose the word from the box that best matches each clue. Write the word on the line.

_____ 9. It's what a piano makes.

_____ 10. It's a group of sailors.

_____ 11. It's what you sweep with.

_____ 12. It's one of the states in the United States.

_____ 13. It's a real gem.

_____ 14. It's how you get ice cream.

_____ 15. It's what the artist did.

_____ 16. It's what a good joke has.

_____ 17. It's all ahead of you.

_____ 18. It means "commonly."

_____ 19. It's what you do when you vote.

_____ 20. It's what the pitcher did.

Notes for Home: Your child spelled words that have the vowel sounds heard in *rule* spelled *oo* and *ew (school, threw)*, *use* spelled *u (music)*, and *off* spelled *augh* and *au (taught, laundry)*. **Home Activity:** Write the spelling words without the vowels. Ask your child to correct them.

Spelling: Consonant Sounds /j/ and /k/

Pretest Directions: Fold back the page along the dotted line. On the blanks, write the spelling words as they are dictated. When you have finished the test, unfold the page and check your words.

1._____

2._____

3._____

4._____

5._____

6._____

7._____

8._____

9._____

10._____

11._____

12._____

13._____

14._____

15._____

16._____

17._____

18._____

19._____

20._____

1. Her father is an Army **major**.

2. Yolanda's best **subject** is math.

3. He is a **junior** camp counselor.

4. The **judge** banged her gavel.

5. We stayed at a mountain **lodge**.

6. The **ridge** is very high.

7. The window **ledge** is icy.

8. The **legend** was interesting.

9. A **general** commands troops.

10. Peaches are grown in **Georgia**.

11. A good **character** is important.

12. Rachel joined the **chorus**.

13. The **orchestra** plays today.

14. He is a good **mechanic**.

15. This is a hard **chord** to play.

16. A **raccoon** ate our food.

17. When did the accident **occur**?

18. This clock is not **accurate**.

19. Do you fish on **occasion**?

20. Did they **accuse** him?

Notes for Home: Your child took a pretest on words that have the consonant sounds of /j/ and /k/. **Home Activity:** Help your child learn misspelled words before the final test. Your child should look at the word, say it, spell it aloud, and then spell it with eyes shut.

Spelling: Consonant Sounds /j/ and /k/

Word List			
major	ridge	character	raccoon
subject	ledge	chorus	occur
junior	legend	orchestra	accurate
judge	general	mechanic	occasion
lodge	Georgia	chord	accuse

Directions: Choose the words from the box that have the consonant sound /k/ heard at the beginning of **car.** Write each word in the correct column.

Consonant /k/ spelled ch

1. _____
2. _____
3. _____
4. _____
5. _____

Consonant /k/ spelled cc

6. _____
7. _____
8. _____
9. _____
10. _____

Directions: Write the word from the box that belongs in each group of words.
Hint: Each word has the consonant sound /j/ heard at the beginning of **jail.**

11. freshman, sophomore, _____

12. Alabama, Mississippi, _____

13. regular, common, _____

14. myth, story, _____

15. greater, important, _____

16. hill, mountain, _____

17. topic, theme, _____

18. inn, hotel, _____

19. lawyer, jury, _____

20. edge, cliff, _____

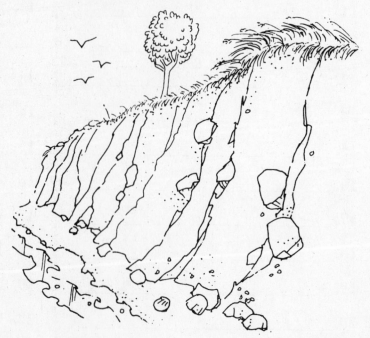

Notes for Home: Your child spelled words that have the consonant sounds /j/ *(junior, ridge, general)* or /k/ *(character, occur).* **Home Activity:** Help your child think of and spell additional words with these sounds and spellings. Then check the spellings in the dictionary.

Spelling: Consonant Sounds /j/ and /k/

Directions: Proofread this report. Find four spelling mistakes. Use the proofreading marks to correct each mistake.

Dolphins are the subjeck of my report. It is not acurate to call dolphins fish. They are actually mammals. Dolphins are warm-blooded and have lungs like other mammals. They are highly intelligent and in general are friendly and playful with humans. On one ocassion, I saw dolphins put on a show in the ocean. Several of them made clicking sounds together like a corus. This is how dolphins communicate.

≡	Make a capital.
/	Make a small letter.
∧	Add something.
ℐ	Take out something.
⊙	Add a period.
¶	Begin a new paragraph.

Spelling Tip

chorus   orchestra
The consonant sound /k/ can be spelled **ch, c,** or **cc.** Remember: You can **hear** the **ch**orus and or**ch**estra.

Word List

major	lodge	general	orchestra	occur
subject	ridge	Georgia	mechanic	accurate
junior	ledge	character	chord	occasion
judge	legend	chorus	raccoon	accuse

Write a Factual Paragraph

On a separate sheet of paper, write a paragraph about a sea animal or a fish. Try to use at least four of your spelling words.

Notes for Home: Your child spelled words that have the consonant sounds /j/ (*junior, ridge, general*) or /k/ (*character, occur*). **Home Activity:** Hold a spelling bee with your child, family, and friends using these spelling words.

Name_____

Spelling: Consonant Sounds /j/ and /k/

REVIEW

Word List

major	ridge	character	raccoon
subject	ledge	chorus	occur
junior	legend	orchestra	accurate
judge	general	mechanic	occasion
lodge	Georgia	chord	accuse

Directions: Choose the word from the box that answers each question. Write the word on the line.

_____ 1. In what state are peaches and peanuts grown?

_____ 2. Who decides who wins a contest?

_____ 3. What animal appears to wear a mask?

_____ 4. Which word can mean both "widespread" and "a commanding officer"?

_____ 5. What group plays music?

_____ 6. What would add to your name if you were named after your father?

_____ 7. What rhymes with *lord* and refers to something musical?

_____ 8. In what kind of building might you stay on a skiing vacation?

Directions: Choose the word from the box that contains each word below. Write the word on the line. Use each word only once.

9. rid _____

10. act _____

11. use _____

12. rate _____

13. sub _____

14. us _____

15. or _____

16. end _____

17. me _____

18. edge _____

19. as _____

20. cur _____

Notes for Home: Your child spelled words that have the consonant sounds /j/ *(junior, ridge, general)* or /k/ *(character, occur)*. **Home Activity:** Take turns picking a spelling word and giving clues about it like those above. Another person must guess the word and spell it.

WR / SR

WEEKLY READER®

The Chocolate WAR

Mombi Bakayoko, 5, uses a machete to cut down cacao pods on a plantation in Ivory Coast.

Fighting to End Slavery on Cacao Farms

THE REAL THREA

People in North Korea call Kim Jong Il the "Great Leader." Outside North Korea, however, many people see him as a bit of an oddball.

Kim wears elevator shoes to make himself look taller than his real height of 5 feet 3 inches. He loves movies, especially James Bond and *Friday the 13th* flicks.

To boost his image, Kim tells schoolchildren that he was born under a double rainbow on North Korea's highest mountain while birds sang and a bright star appeared in the sky. The truth is, he was born in Russia, where his father was living at the time.

Kim's favorite cartoon character: Daffy Duck.

For sure, it is easy to dismiss Kim as off-the-wall. Some reporters laughingly call him "Dr. Evil," after the twisted character in the *Austin Powers* movies.

It's no joke, however, that Kim is trying

to make communist North Korea—an Asian country with 22 million people and fewer square miles than Mississippi—a world nuclear power. The strategy is a source of dire concern for the United States and many of its allies.

Kim Jong Il reviews a military exercise in North Korea.

Long-Range Missile

Last month, the Central Intelligence Agency (CIA) sounded the latest alarm about Kim and North Korea. The CIA said it had proof that North Korea has a missile that, if launched, could soar across the Pacific Ocean and strike the west coast of the United States.

Only a few months earlier, the United States learned that Kim had broken an international agreement by secretly gathering materials

to build n weapons.

Althoug North K long-rang sile has n tested, son governmer cials are w Such a n fitted w nuclear warhead would serious risk to North Ame

Power Monger?

Why would North Kore to build a nuclear arsena answer may lie with Kim quest for power.

Kim took control of

A South Kore stands ready ne display of missiles

Inset: NewsCom

—NewsCom

North Korean soldiers march in Pyongyang, the capital of North Korea. North Korea has one of the largest armies in the world.

—NewsCom

Korea in
after Kim Il
his father, died.
der Kim earned
t as a war hero
g World War II
—1945) and as a
s leader after the
He ruled North
for 46 years.
younger Kim
such repu-
but
ng a
military
top priority.
a drought led to the star-
of 2 million North
ns, the dictator still
money into his military.
ay, Kim is in charge of
the largest armies in
orld. North Korea has
llion active troops and
llion reserves.
th Korea also has 200
-range missiles capable
king targets in neighbor-

ing South Korea and Japan.

There is also evidence that Kim has chemical and biological weapons that could harm millions of people. Many of North Korea's neighbors are on edge, especially South Korea.

U.S. Response

The United States is keeping a close eye on Kim and North Korea, although its attention in recent months has been on Saddam Hussein and Iraq.

President George W. Bush lumps North Korea with Iraq and Iran in terms of threats to world peace. He has called the three nations the "Axis of Evil."

A reporter for *The Washington Post* once asked Bush his opinion of North Korea's leader. Bush replied, "I loathe Kim Jong Il!"

Playing With Fire

Although wary of North Korea, the Bush administration has made it clear that it considers Saddam Hussein a bigger threat than Kim.

However, some critics say Bush is foolish to ignore North Korea. They say a fully armed North Korea has a greater chance of wreaking havoc on the world than Iraq ever could.

One Bush administration official told *Newsweek* magazine that Kim is used to having things his way.

Most people can agree that the world hasn't heard the last from Kim. WR

RUSSIA
Yalu River
NORTH KOREA
SEA OF JAPAN
Pyongyang
Demilitarized Zone
Seoul
SOUTH KOREA
JAPAN
Korea Strait

—Leigh Haeger

Critical Thinking

How do you think the United States should handle North Korea?

—PictureQuest

Choi
W

What would life be like without rich, creamy, lip-smacking, mouthwatering, melt-in-your-mouth chocolate?

Life would be bitter for most Americans. They spend about $13 billion a year buying all sorts of chocolate treats, from chocolate brownies to chocolate bars.

However, for the African children who toil under slavelike conditions on *cacao* plantations, life isn't so sweet. The cacao bean is the main ingredient in chocolate.

According to a 2002 survey by the International Institute of Tropical Agriculture and the U.S. Agency for International Development, an estimated 284,000 children work in dangerous conditions on cacao farms in western Africa.

More than half of these children are under 14 years old. Many were sold into forced labor to work 12 hours or more a day on the cacao plantations. The rest of the children work as laborers on family-run farms.

Because the children spend so many hours working, they can't go to school.

"These children are not only working in dangerous jobs, they are also losing the chance for an education," said U.S. Deputy Under Secretary for International Affairs Tom Moorhead.

Officials in Ivory Coast arrested cacao grower Lenikpo Yeo for failing to pay 19 child laborers for their work.

Helping Growers

A number of international organizations, including several African governments, recently began a program to eliminate child labor on cacao plantations.

Under the program, government officials will remove children from abusive work situations while teaching farm about child labor issues.

The program will also mak easier for cacao growers to b row money. Officials h farmers will use the borrow money to invest in their far

Harvesting Cacao

—Agnes Moya; NewsCom; All others: AP Wide World Photos

Using a machete, Gambi Gbanble cuts a pod from a cacao tree (far left). Workers must split the pod to get at the cacao beans (second from left). Workers, such as Agnes Moya, then dry the beans in the sun (second from right). Once bagged, the beans are shipped to chocolate makers.

icials hope that if the farms
a *profit*, or make money, the
wers can pay workers a
ent wage instead of relying
child labor.

he program will also send
hers into the homes of child
rers to make sure the chil-
receive an education.

er Taste of Slavery

years, the use of children as
es in the cacao fields of
y Coast, Cameroon, Ghana,
other African countries
ained a well-guarded secret.
he low price of cacao forced
ers to cut costs to maintain
fits. The growers, unable to
workers, used children to
the beans. The growers usu-
tricked or threatened children
working on the farms.

Poverty can propel people to
tic measures to survive, and
sequently, children are vic-
ized in the process," said
ta Sheth, of the humanitarian
p Save the Children.

2001, journalists exposed
horrific details of the chil-

dren's lives. Chocolate makers
then decided to try and stop the
brutality of child labor on the
cacao farms.

One 12-year-old boy told a
reporter of the harsh treatment
he received at the hands of one
cacao grower.

"He tied me behind my back
with rope and beat me with
a piece of wood," the boy said.
"Then he took a small gun and
said, 'I'm going to kill you
and dump you in a well.'"

Moving Too Slowly?

The chocolate industry,
with the support of the
U.S. government and
world labor organizations,
has established a plan to help
end child labor on the cacao
plantations by 2005.

Critics, however, charge
that the companies who
purchase the cacao
beans to make
chocolate products
are moving too
slow in abolishing
child slavery.
They say thou-
sands of African
children continue
to work from dawn
to dusk to pick
the cacao beans.

The chocolate
manufacturers
say their compa-
nies are doing all
they can to help.
But there are

problems. For example, a civil
war in Ivory Coast—the largest
producer of cacao—is making it
hard to help the children.

Mohammed Maigo, who
works as a government official
in the small African country
of Mali, hopes that the children
working on the cacao plantations
soon have a better life.

"The blood of African
children is in our bars of chocolate." he said. ⓌⓇ

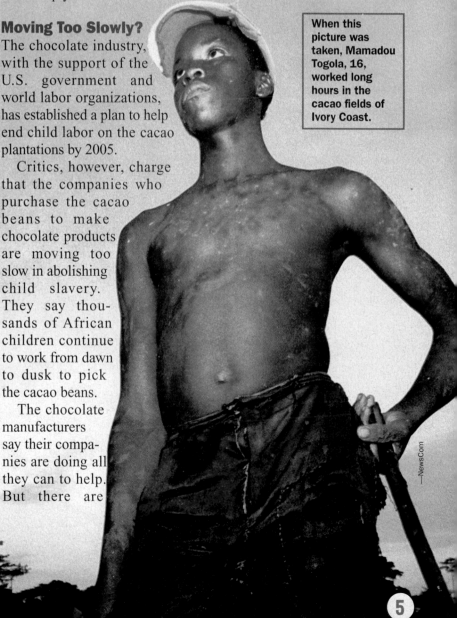

When this
picture was
taken, Mamadou
Togola, 16,
worked long
hours in the
cacao fields of
Ivory Coast.

—NewsCom

⑤

Beyond the Shuttle

An elevator to space? A spaceship with engines so powerful that the vehicle can take off like an airplane and fly—not blast off—into orbit?

Though those ideas may sound like the basis of an episode of *Star Trek: The Next Generation*, the National Aeronautics and Space Administration (NASA) is currently working on a series of space-craft that might include such vehicles.

On the top of NASA's list is a space taxi that would ferry ten astronauts at a time to and from the *International Space Station* (ISS) beginning in 2010. NASA is spending $882 million to design the craft called the *Orbital Space Plane*.

The space plane is a shuttlelike craft that would sit on top of a rocket. The rocket would blast the plane into orbit.

"It would not be a space shuttle replacement," Barry Davidson of Syracuse University said of the space plane. "It would be the next-generation vehicle out there."

Within the next 15 or so years, scientists say, NASA will have to replace the three remaining space shuttles—*Discovery*, *Atlantis*, and *Endeavour*—which were all built in the 1970s and early 1980s.

NASA might replace the shuttles with a space-craft that would be attached to the back of a larger

This planned spacecraft will ride piggyback on a larger aircraft.

aircraft, such as the one illustrated in the i below. Once both vehicles are airborne, the sp craft would release itself and speed into c using a super-powerful jet engine called a *ra* or a *scramjet*.

The ramjet or scramjet engine would prope craft into orbit at ten times the speed of so Sound travels through air at 1,087 feet per ond. Engineers will test an unpiloted 12- scramjet-powered craft, the *X-43*, later this yea

Still, scientists say the eas way to get into space might jus by elevator. NASA scientists currently working on a plan would put a large satellite in 22,300 miles above the equa The satellite would be program to constantly hover over the s spot on Earth's surface.

Scientists would attach to satellite a very long cable and an elevator could then be used to transport people and e ment up into space.

"We think we can have it up and operati in about 15 years," said scientist Bradle Edwards.

The *Orbital Space Plane*, pictured below, will be able to ferry astronauts to the *International Space Station*.

Harry Potter AND THE ORDER OF THE PHOENIX

K. Rowling

Here's a riddle that even a muggle could answer: Can a book nobody has read become a bestseller? It can when that book is the in author J.K. Rowling's *Harry Potter* series. *arry Potter and the Order of the Phoenix* 't arrive in stores until June 21. Even so, orders he novel have sent it to the top of at least two seller lists. Demand for the book is so great its publisher ordered a record-setting first ing of 6.8 million copies. And that's just in the ed States!

owling's previous book, *Harry Potter and the let of Fire*, sold out its first 3.8 million copies in two days. The cover price for the next *y Potter* book is $29.99. The book will con- a whopping 896 pages of adventures.

he first four *Harry Potter* books have sold ly 80 million copies in the United States.

Dear Senior Edition,
    I really liked the article "Rodent Racers" [issue 17]. I really liked this article because I would love to a pet rat running a race and jumping hurdles. I that's cool because I used to jump hurdles in sec- nd third grades. I was in the newspaper, too.
—Rebecca M., P.S. 107, Brooklyn, N.Y.

Senior Edition,
eally liked the article "Who Sank the *Bismarck*?" 18] because I had never heard of the ship before. I know that ships like the *Bismarck* could be so awe- . I think it would be scary to sink to the bottom of the ic Ocean.
—Tasha B., Ben Franklin Elementary School, Vancouver, Wash.

 to us! Tell us what YOU think about any story in *y Reader* Senior Edition. Include your name, school, and state. Write to
 Said It!
ekly Reader Senior Edition
0 First Stamford Place
. Box 120023
amford, CT 06912-0023 or send e-mail to
nior@weeklyreader.com.

Mystery Photo

This mystery photo kind of grows on you. What is this a mystery photo of?

The Simpsons turns 300

300 Big Ones!

—FOX

"Remember," Homer Simpson once told his cartoon family, "as far as anyone knows, we are a nice, normal family."

Although they're not really normal, everyone seems to love *The Simpsons*. The series recently celebrated its 300th episode, a huge milestone by television standards. Now in its 14th season, *The Simpsons* is poised to replace *The Adventures of Ozzie and Harriet* as the longest-running situation comedy in television history. *The Adventures of Ozzie and Harriet*, about a family named the Nelsons, ran from 1952 to 1966.

The Simpsons made its debut on January 14, 1990. Fox has ordered two more seasons of the show, which will move *The Simpsons* ahead of *Ozzie and Harriet* as the longest-running comedy ever to appear on television. Moreover, *The Simpsons* is regularly the top-rated show on Sundays with viewers ages 18 to 49, as well as with teens. The show is the most honored animated series in television history, garnering 18 Emmys and other awards.

As the evil Mr. Burns might say, "Excellent."

Name:

Know the News

Fill in the oval in front of the correct answer.

1. How much money do Americans spend each year on chocolate products?
   - Ⓐ $2.5 million
   - Ⓑ $13 million
   - Ⓒ $13 billion

2. According to a 2002 survey by the International Institute of Tropical Agriculture and the U.S. Agency for International Development, how many children work in dangerous conditions on cacao farms?
   - Ⓐ 284,000
   - Ⓑ 456,000
   - Ⓒ 594,000

3. Which country was Kim Jong Il born?
   - Ⓐ North Korea
   - Ⓑ Russia
   - Ⓒ China

4. How many Emmy Awards has *The Simpsons* won?
   - Ⓐ 10
   - Ⓑ 12
   - Ⓒ 18

What's the Word?

Fill in the oval in front of the word or phrase that means about the same as each numbered word below. The page number indicates where the word is used in this issue.

1. **quest** (noun, page 2)
   - Ⓐ search
   - Ⓑ place
   - Ⓒ name

2. **havoc** (noun, page 3)
   - Ⓐ hinge
   - Ⓑ order
   - Ⓒ disorder

3. **ingredient** (noun, page 4)
   - Ⓐ search for information
   - Ⓑ part of a mixture
   - Ⓒ anticipated amount

4. **harsh** (adjective, page 5)
   - Ⓐ demanding
   - Ⓑ proud
   - Ⓒ selfish

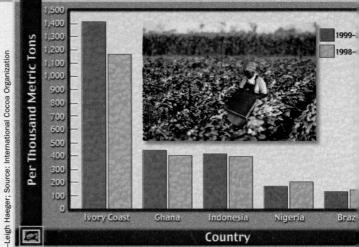

Main Cacao–Producing Countri

Per Thousand Metric Tons

—Leigh Haeger; Source: International Cocoa Organization

1999–
1998–

Ivory Coast   Ghana   Indonesia   Nigeria   Braz

Country

Read the Graph

Fill in the oval in front of the correct answer.

1. According to the graph, approximately how much cacao did Ivory Coast produce in 1998–1999?
   - Ⓐ 1,400,000 metric tons
   - Ⓑ 1,150,000 metric tons
   - Ⓒ 773,000 metric tons

2. How many countries produced less than 300 metric tons of cacao in 1999–2000?
   - Ⓐ two
   - Ⓑ three
   - Ⓒ five

3. Approximately how much cacao did Brazil pr duce in 1999–2000?
   - Ⓐ 40,000 metric tons
   - Ⓑ 56,000 metric tons
   - Ⓒ 150,000 metric tons

4. Which two countries listed below produced l cacao in 1999–2000 than in 1998–1999?
   - Ⓐ Ivory Coast and Nigeria
   - Ⓑ Nigeria and Brazil
   - Ⓒ Indonesia and Ghana

Check out *Weekly Reader* Galaxy on the World Wide Web for updates on stories in this issue, games, contests, and more! **www.weeklyreader.com**

Spelling: Words with *kn*, *mb*, *gh*, *st*

Pretest Directions: Fold back the page along the dotted line. On the blanks, write the spelling words as they are dictated. When you have finished the test, unfold the page and check your words.

1._____

2._____

3._____

4._____

5._____

6._____

7._____

8._____

9._____

10._____

11._____

12._____

13._____

14._____

15._____

16._____

17._____

18._____

19._____

20._____

1. Her **knowledge** is very great.

2. I **know** many people.

3. No one **knew** how to do it.

4. He cracked his **knuckle**.

5. Grandmother is **knitting**.

6. This **knapsack** is very large.

7. My feet are cold and **numb**.

8. The team defused the **bomb**.

9. This **tomb** is ancient.

10. The **climber** scaled the cliff.

11. **Plumbing** is a hard job.

12. He thought he saw a **ghost**.

13. We ate **spaghetti** for lunch.

14. They were **aghast** at the idea.

15. The wet stones **glisten**.

16. Are you **listening** to me?

17. **Fasten** your seatbelts.

18. They **hustle** down the hall.

19. **Mistletoe** lives on trees.

20. Can you **whistle** a tune?

Notes for Home: Your child took a pretest on words that include the letters *kn, mb, gh,* and *st.*
Home Activity: Help your child learn misspelled words before the final test. Your child can underline the word parts that caused the problems and concentrate on those parts.

Think and Practice

Spelling: Words with *kn*, *mb*, *gh*, *st*

Word List				
knowledge	knitting	tomb	spaghetti	fasten
know	knapsack	climber	aghast	hustle
knew	numb	plumbing	glisten	mistletoe
knuckle	bomb	ghost	listening	whistle

Directions: Choose the words from the box that either begin or end with a silent consonant. Write each word in the correct column.

Begins with a Silent Consonant

1. _____
2. _____
3. _____
4. _____
5. _____
6. _____

Ends with a Silent Consonant

7. _____
8. _____
9. _____

Directions: Choose the word from the box that best completes each sentence. Write the word on the line to the left.

_____ 10. Always _____ your seat belt when riding in a car.

_____ 11. The _____ plant has small, waxy white berries and green leaves.

_____ 12. The _____ reached the snowy mountaintop.

_____ 13. We have leaky _____ in our house.

_____ 14. My favorite meal is _____ and meatballs.

_____ 15. We didn't have a _____ of a chance of winning.

_____ 16. They had to _____ to make the early train.

_____ 17. His parents were _____ at his bad grades.

_____ 18. "Are you _____ to me?" asked the teacher.

_____ 19. Sweat will _____ on your skin when you exercise.

_____ 20. Does your dog come when you _____?

Notes for Home: Your child spelled words with *kn*, *mb*, *gh*, and *st* in which the two letters together stand for only one sound. ***Home Activity:*** Help your child think of and spell additional words that have the letters *mb* and *st* where the *b* and *t* are silent, such as *comb*, *limb* and *wrestle*.

Spelling: Words with *kn, mb, gh, st*

Directions: Proofread this letter. Find five spelling mistakes. Use the proofreading marks to correct each mistake.

☰	Make a capital.
╱	Make a small letter.
∧	Add something.
⸦	Take out something.
⊙	Add a period.
⁊	Begin a new paragraph.

Dear Dan,

Last night a tornado hit our area. I knew something was wrong when I heard the wind whisle loudly. My mom was lissening to the radio. She stopped her nitting and told me to fastten the door. We spent the night in the cellar. I was num with fear.

Aren't you glad you live in another state?

Your friend,

Mark

Spelling Tip

Sometimes two consonants together stand for one sound. Remember to keep the **k** when spelling words with **kn**.

Word List

knowledge	plumbing
know	ghost
knew	spaghetti
knuckle	aghast
knitting	glisten
knapsack	listening
numb	fasten
bomb	hustle
tomb	mistletoe
climber	whistle

Write a Letter

On a separate sheet of paper, write a letter that Dan might send back to Mark. Describe a natural disaster that Dan experienced, such as a flood or blizzard. Try to use at least five of your spelling words.

Notes for Home: You child spelled words that have *kn, mb, gh,* or *st* in which the two letters together stand for only one sound. *Home Activity:* Say each word aloud. Have your child spell it and tell you which consonant is silent.

Spelling: Words with *kn, mb, gh, st*

Word List				
knowledge	knitting	tomb	spaghetti	fasten
know	knapsack	climber	aghast	hustle
knew	numb	plumbing	glisten	mistletoe
knuckle	bomb	ghost	listening	whistle

Directions: Choose the word from the box that best matches each clue. Write the word on the line.

_____ **1.** Anything that is dim, pale, or shadowy is like this.

_____ **2.** This kind of noodle can be fun to eat.

_____ **3.** If you like sewing, you might like this too.

_____ **4.** This brings water to your kitchen sink.

_____ **5.** This person is always going up or down.

_____ **6.** Some students should do less talking and more of this.

_____ **7.** An Egyptian pyramid is an example of this.

_____ **8.** By studying, you get more of this every year.

Directions: Write the word from the box that belongs in each group.

 9. sparkle, shine, _____

10. understand, think, _____

11. to flop, to fail, to _____

12. plant, white berries, _____

13. zip, button, _____

14. backpack, bookbag, _____

15. elbow, wrist, _____

16. cold, stiff, _____

17. hum, sing, _____

18. horrified, terrified, _____

19. realized, understood, _____

20. hurry, rush, _____

Notes for Home: Your child spelled words that have the letters *kn, mb, gh,* and *st* in which the two letters together stand for only one sound. *Home Activity:* Make a crossword puzzle with your child using words from the box. Decide where the words will intersect. Then write clues.

Spelling: Compound Words 1

Pretest Directions: Fold back the page along the dotted line. On the blanks, write the spelling words as they are dictated. When you have finished the test, unfold the page and check your words.

1._____
2._____
3._____
4._____
5._____
6._____
7._____
8._____
9._____
10._____
11._____
12._____
13._____
14._____
15._____
16._____
17._____
18._____
19._____
20._____

1. The **mailbox** is full.
2. There are many stores **nearby**.
3. We went **into** the library.
4. **Sometimes** I forget to be polite.
5. It was a beautiful **sunset**.
6. Is there **anything** I can do?
7. It was broad **daylight**.
8. Did you hear **something**?
9. Carl needs a **haircut**.
10. I lost my **notebook**.
11. The **earthquake** was scary.
12. The bandits have a **hideout**.
13. Read your history **textbook**.
14. We played **volleyball** today.
15. **Horseback** riding is fun.
16. Renaldo has neat **handwriting**.
17. My bike's **kickstand** broke.
18. The **rattlesnake** almost bit me.
19. This **fireplace** is made of stone.
20. **Housework** can be tiring.

Notes for Home: Your child took a pretest on compound words. *Home Activity:* Help your child learn misspelled words before the final test. Dictate the word and have your child spell the word aloud for you or write it on paper.

Spelling: Compound Words 1

Word List

mailbox	sunset	haircut	textbook	kickstand
nearby	anything	notebook	volleyball	rattlesnake
into	daylight	earthquake	horseback	fireplace
sometimes	something	hideout	handwriting	housework

Directions: Combine a word from each box below to form a compound word from the word list. Write the compound word on the line.

some	back
note	quake
some	out
hide	place
horse	thing
kick	stand
earth	times
rattle	book
fire	snake

1. _____

2. _____

3. _____

4. _____

5. _____

6. _____

7. _____

8. _____

9. _____

Directions: Find two words in each sentence that make up a compound word from the box. Write the word on the line.

_____ **10.** Our house needs a lot of work done to it.

_____ **11.** It took just a single volley for the ball to go out.

_____ **12.** I looked in the cupboard to see what was left.

_____ **13.** He dropped the piece of mail in the box.

_____ **14.** Isn't there any way I can give this thing back?

_____ **15.** We watched the sun as it set in the sky.

_____ **16.** During the day, the light is very bright.

_____ **17.** It is near the stream that runs by our house.

_____ **18.** I wrote the text for the book, but I didn't illustrate it.

_____ **19.** My hand is sore from writing.

_____ **20.** My hair is long, and I need to get it cut.

Notes for Home: Your child spelled compound words, longer words formed by joining two or more shorter words. *Home Activity:* Together, see how many items you can find in your home that have names that are compound words. List them, and check a dictionary.

Name_____

Spelling: Compound Words 1

Directions: Proofread this advertisement. Find four spelling mistakes. Use the proofreading marks to correct each mistake.

Volunteers Wanted!

Are you a young person looking for somethin to do this summer? Shady Rest Home is looking for young people who live nearbye to spend a few hours a week with our residents. We need volunteers to read, play voleyball and other games, or just visit and talk. Sometimes you might be needed to help in the kitchen or do some light housewerk. If interested, call 555-3725 or drop a note into a mailbox today.

≡	Make a capital.
/	Make a small letter.
∧	Add something.
ℐ	Take out something.
⊙	Add a period.
¶	Begin a new paragraph.

Spelling Tip

Remember to keep all the letters of the shorter words when spelling compound words. For example: **hide + out = hideout.**

Word List

mailbox	earthquake
nearby	hideout
into	textbook
sometimes	volleyball
sunset	horseback
anything	handwriting
daylight	kickstand
something	rattlesnake
haircut	fireplace
notebook	housework

Write an Advertisement

On a separate sheet of paper, write your own advertisement offering a service or selling a product. Try to use at least four of your spelling words.

Notes for Home: Your child spelled compound words, longer words formed by joining two or more shorter words. *Home Activity:* Look at the words in the box that your child didn't use in his or her writing exercise. Ask him or her to use several of these words in a sentence.

Spelling: Compound Words 1   31

Spelling: Compound Words 1

REVIEW

Word List

mailbox	anything	earthquake	handwriting
nearby	daylight	hideout	kickstand
into	something	textbook	rattlesnake
sometimes	haircut	volleyball	fireplace
sunset	notebook	horseback	housework

Directions: Write the word from the box that is associated with each place.

1. stationery store _____

2. barbershop _____

3. post office _____

4. school _____

5. stable _____

6. sports shop _____

7. bicycle shop _____

8. desert _____

Directions: Choose the word from the box that best completes each sentence.
Write the word on the line to the left.

_____ 9. Many homes were destroyed by the _____.

_____ 10. All that was left standing of one house was the brick _____.

_____ 11. Rebecca wanted to do _____ to help the victims.

_____ 12. She filled out an application in her best _____.

_____ 13. She awoke at _____ to join the group of volunteers.

_____ 14. They scoured the disaster area looking for anyone concealed in a _____.

_____ 15. She shone her flashlight _____ dark spaces and holes.

_____ 16. She listened carefully but didn't hear _____.

_____ 17. _____ she felt like giving up.

_____ 18. Then several children were located in a _____ basement.

_____ 19. By _____ Rebecca was exhausted.

_____ 20. She couldn't even think of the _____ that would be needed to get these homes back in order.

Notes for Home: Your child spelled compound words, longer words formed by joining two or more shorter words, such as *housework* and *fireplace*. **Home Activity:** Challenge your child to make up a story using as many of the compound words listed above as possible.

Spelling: Short Vowels *a, i, o, u*

Pretest Directions: Fold back the page along the dotted line. On the blanks, write the spelling words as they are dictated. When you have finished the test, unfold the page and check your words.

1._____	**1.** The pump **handle** is loose.
2._____	**2. Perhaps** they will not come.
3._____	**3.** Please control your **anger**.
4._____	**4.** There was an auto **accident**.
5._____	**5.** Traveling can be an **adventure**.
6._____	**6.** We will finish **before** them.
7._____	**7.** She cried **because** she was sad.
8._____	**8.** Have you **decided** what to do?
9._____	**9.** Let's **pretend** to be airplanes.
10._____	**10.** The clothes **belong** to Sue.
11._____	**11.** Is it really **possible**?
12._____	**12.** Detectives might **solve** the case.
13._____	**13.** This is a hard math **problem**.
14._____	**14.** Sarah likes to eat **lobster**.
15._____	**15.** The **python** is a large snake.
16._____	**16.** The monkey **swung** in the tree.
17._____	**17.** The **jungle** was full of noises.
18._____	**18.** The space **shuttle** took off.
19._____	**19.** I hate the sight of **blood**.
20._____	**20.** The **flood** caused damage.

Notes for Home: Your child took a pretest on words that have the short vowels *a, i, o,* and *u*. *Home Activity:* Help your child learn misspelled words before the final test. Have your child divide misspelled words into parts (such as syllables) and concentrate on each part.

Spelling: Short Vowels *a, i, o, u*

Word List			
handle	before	possible	swung
perhaps	because	solve	jungle
anger	decided	problem	shuttle
accident	pretend	lobster	blood
adventure	belong	python	flood

Directions: Choose the words from the box that have the **short u** sound heard in **sun** or the **short i** sound heard in **begin.** Write each word in the correct column.

Short u spelled u

1. _____

2. _____

3. _____

Short u spelled oo

4. _____

5. _____

Short i spelled e

6. _____

7. _____

8. _____

9. _____

10. _____

Directions: Choose the word from the box that best replaces the underlined word or words. Write the word on the line.

_____ 11. We took in our new dog, Flash, purely by <u>chance</u>.

_____ 12. Getting him home was an <u>exciting, dangerous experience</u>.

_____ 13. My sister pinched him so hard putting on his collar, he must have thought she was a <u>hard-shelled sea animal</u>.

_____ 14. She quickly learned to <u>control</u> the dog gently.

_____ 15. My brother gave Flash a squeeze like a <u>big, thick snake</u>.

_____ 16. Our cat, though, presents a serious <u>dilemma</u>.

_____ 17. Fluff still has moments of <u>rage</u> about sharing our attention.

_____ 18. <u>Maybe</u> Flash and Fluff will get along well soon.

_____ 19. It's not <u>impossible</u> that a cat and dog can be friends.

_____ 20. With a little training and separate rooms, we will <u>figure out</u> this difficulty.

Notes for Home: Your child spelled words that have the short vowel sounds *a, i, o,* or *u* (*handle, before, possible, swung, good*). **Home Activity:** Say these words with your child and look at how the vowel sounds are spelled. Add other words that have the same vowel sounds and spellings.

Spelling: Short Vowels *a, i, o, u*

Directions: Proofread this article. Find five spelling mistakes. Use the proofreading marks to correct each mistake.

For many years the Everglades were in danger of being destroyed. Then the people of Florida desided to solve the problum before it was too late.

Water that had been dammed up was allowed to flud into the area. Underpasses were built so wild animals could travel safely under highways. Exotic plants that didn't bilong there were removed bicuz they choked out native plants. These solutions helped save the Everglades.

☰	Make a capital.
∕	Make a small letter.
∧	Add something.
⌿	Take out something.
⊙	Add a period.
⁋	Begin a new paragraph.

Spelling Tip

blood   flood

The **short u** sound can be spelled **u** or **oo**. Remember to spell **blood** and **flood** with two o's by remembering that liquids can **ooze**.

Word List

handle	possible
perhaps	solve
anger	problem
accident	lobster
adventure	python
before	swung
because	jungle
decided	shuttle
pretend	blood
belong	flood

Write a Science Article

On a separate sheet of paper, write a short article about how people in your community or state are protecting the environment. Try to use at least five of your spelling words.

Notes for Home: Your child spelled words that have the short vowel sounds *a, i, o,* or *u (h<u>a</u>ndle, b<u>e</u>fore, p<u>o</u>ssible, sw<u>u</u>ng, g<u>oo</u>d)*. **Home Activity:** Have your child find other verb forms of *decided, pretend,* and *swung,* such as *deciding, pretended,* and *swing.*

Spelling: Short Vowels *a, i, o, u*

Word List

handle	before	possible	swung
perhaps	because	solve	jungle
anger	decided	problem	shuttle
accident	pretend	lobster	blood
adventure	belong	python	flood

Directions: Choose the word from the box that is the most opposite in meaning for each word or words below. Write the word on the line.

1. impossible _____

2. solution _____

3. after _____

4. real _____

5. drought _____

6. undecided _____

7. joy _____

8. deliberate _____

Directions: Choose the word from the box that best matches each clue. Write the word on the line.

_____ 9. part of a teapot

_____ 10. a tasty shellfish

_____ 11. a fluid in the body

_____ 12. what members do to a club

_____ 13. the past tense of *swing*

_____ 14. a huge kind of snake

_____ 15. the same as *maybe*

_____ 16. found in a rainforest

_____ 17. a bus that runs back and forth

_____ 18. an exciting experience

_____ 19. what detectives do to crimes

_____ 20. why things happen

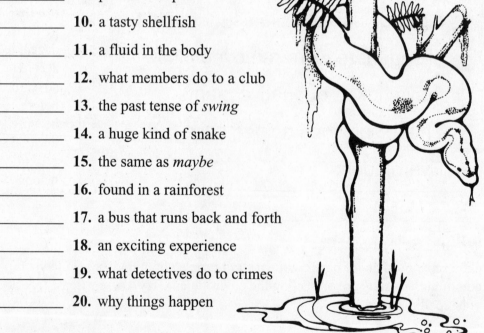

Notes for Home: Your child identified spelling words from opposites and clues. ***Home Activity:*** Challenge your child to write a paragraph using as many spelling words as possible.

Spelling: Prefixes *dis-*, *un-*, *mid-*, and *pre-*

Pretest Directions: Fold back the page along the dotted line. On the blanks, write the spelling words as they are dictated. When you have finished the test, unfold the page and check your words.

1._____

2._____

3._____

4._____

5._____

6._____

7._____

8._____

9._____

10._____

11._____

12._____

13._____

14._____

15._____

16._____

17._____

18._____

19._____

20._____

1. We **discovered** it just in time.

2. The room was in total **disorder**.

3. I am sorry to **disappoint** you.

4. They **disobey** orders.

5. Does she **disapprove** of him?

6. The driver is **unsure** how to go.

7. The writing was too **unclear**.

8. Are you **unable** to help today?

9. You may **unbuckle** your seatbelt.

10. He has an **unlimited** supply.

11. The news came **midweek**.

12. It is time for a **midyear** review.

13. The games are on the **midway**.

14. The bell tower chimed **midnight**.

15. The deer stood in **midstream**.

16. We will have a **pretest** tomorrow.

17. They are too old for **preschool**.

18. The restaurants **precook** meals.

19. We **prepaid** for our tickets.

20. This program was **prerecorded**.

Notes for Home: Your child took a pretest on words that begin with *dis-*, *un-*, *mid-*, and *pre-*.
Home Activity: Help your child learn misspelled words before the final test. See if there are any similar errors and discuss a memory trick that could help.

Name_____

Think and Practice

Spelling: Prefixes *dis-*, *un-*, *mid-*, and *pre-*

Word List

discovered	disapprove	unbuckle	midway	preschool
disorder	unsure	unlimited	midnight	precook
disappoint	unclear	midweek	midstream	prepaid
disobey	unable	midyear	pretest	prerecorded

Directions: Add the prefix **dis-**, **un-**, **mid-**, or **pre-** to each word below to form a word from the box. Write the word on the line.

1. covered _____
2. night _____
3. recorded _____
4. year _____
5. obey _____

6. stream _____
7. approve _____
8. sure _____
9. buckle _____
10. clear _____

Directions: Choose the word from the box that best matches each clue. Write the word in the puzzle.

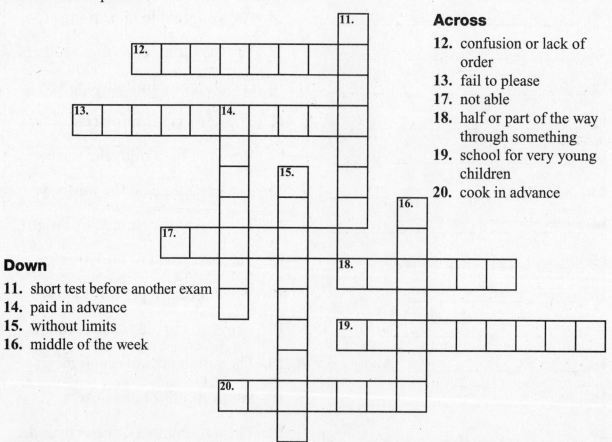

Across

12. confusion or lack of order
13. fail to please
17. not able
18. half or part of the way through something
19. school for very young children
20. cook in advance

Down

11. short test before another exam
14. paid in advance
15. without limits
16. middle of the week

Notes for Home: Your child spelled words that begin with *dis-*, *un-*, *mid-*, and *pre-*. **Home Activity:** Read each word aloud from the box. Ask your child to identify and spell the base word. For example, *buckle* is the base word for *unbuckle*.

38 Spelling: Prefixes *dis-*, *un-*, *mid-*, and *pre-*

Spelling: Prefixes *dis-, un-, mid-, pre-*

Directions: Proofread these rules. Find six spelling mistakes.
Use the proofreading marks to correct each mistake.

≡	Make a capital.
/	Make a small letter.
∧	Add something.
✌	Take out something.
⊙	Add a period.
¶	Begin a new paragraph.

Proofread and Write

Rules for Our Trip to the Shopping Mall

We will be in a big crowd tomorrow at the shopping

mall, so everyone remember these rules!

1. Do not dissobey the instructions of the teacher or the group leader.

If you do, it will cause great disordar.

2. If you have diskovered that you are unnclear about which bus you

belong on, ask the teacher. Space on each bus is not unlimitted, so you

must go on the bus you were assigned.

3. We will eat middway through the day. The lunch is prepaid, so you

don't need to bring any money for food.

We want everyone to have fun, so please remember these rules and be

on time tomorrow!

Spelling Tip

discovered

How can you remember that **discovered**
begins with **disc,** not **disk?** When something
is **discovered,** you can see (**c**) it!

Word List

discovered	midweek
disorder	midyear
disappoint	midway
disobey	midnight
disapprove	midstream
unsure	pretest
unclear	preschool
unable	precook
unbuckle	prepaid
unlimited	prerecorded

Write Rules

Imagine you are in charge of a group that is visiting
a shopping mall. On a separate sheet of paper, make
a list of rules for the group to follow. Try to use at
least five of your spelling words.

Notes for Home: Your child spelled words that begin with *dis-, un-, mid-,* and *pre-*. **Home
Activity:** Read a magazine article with your child. See how many words you can find that start
with the prefixes *dis-, un-, mid-,* or *pre-*.

Name_____

Spelling: Prefixes *dis-, un-, mid-, pre-* REVIEW

Word List				
discovered	disapprove	unbuckle	midway	preschool
disorder	unsure	unlimited	midnight	precook
disappoint	unclear	midweek	midstream	prepaid
disobey	unable	midyear	pretest	prerecorded

Directions: Choose the word from the box that best completes each sentence.
Write the word on the line.

_____ 1. When I was in _____ I was too young to work at our family store.

_____ 2. _____ through the fifth grade I began to help my parents at the store.

_____ 3. I soon _____ that I enjoyed stocking the shelves.

_____ 4. After school I wanted to straighten the items that were in _____.

_____ 5. I would never _____ when my parents asked me to complete a task.

_____ 6. Mother was _____ to hide a smile at her delight in my contribution to the store.

_____ 7. If I was _____ about how to do something, mother helped.

_____ 8. My love for helping at the store was endless and _____.

Directions: Choose the word from the box that has the same or nearly the same meaning as each word or phrase below. Write the word on the line.

_____ 9. twelve o'clock A.M.   _____ 15. already paid

_____ 10. Wednesday   _____ 16. unfasten

_____ 11. June   _____ 17. taped

_____ 12. frown on   _____ 18. doubtful

_____ 13. quiz   _____ 19. let down

_____ 14. middle of the stream   _____ 20. preheat

Notes for Home: Your child spelled words that begin with *dis-, un-, mid-,* and *pre-*. **Home Activity:** Name one of these prefixes: *dis-, un-, mid-,* or *pre-*. Have your child identify the spelling words that begin with that prefix, and have him or her write a sentence for each one.

Spelling: Adding -s and -es

Pretest Directions: Fold back the page along the dotted line. On the blanks, write the spelling words as they are dictated. When you have finished the test, unfold the page and check your words.

1._____	**1.** It takes **months** to do this.
2._____	**2.** Wes will miss his old **friends**.
3._____	**3.** Study to improve your **grades**.
4._____	**4.** **Cowboys** ride horses.
5._____	**5.** The **valleys** are green and grassy.
6._____	**6.** **Donkeys** pulled the hay cart.
7._____	**7.** **Missiles** are dangerous.
8._____	**8.** Sew the **costumes** for the play.
9._____	**9.** These **pictures** are good.
10._____	**10.** Most **mornings**, he takes the bus.
11._____	**11.** Corey's tie **matches** his socks.
12._____	**12.** Daria hid in the **bushes**.
13._____	**13.** Fans watched from the **benches**.
14._____	**14.** Nobody listens to her **speeches**.
15._____	**15.** Did you check their hall **passes**?
16._____	**16.** His mom **kisses** him goodbye.
17._____	**17.** **Dresses** come in many colors.
18._____	**18.** My **batteries** are running low.
19._____	**19.** **Companies** give people jobs.
20._____	**20.** It's been done for **centuries**.

Notes for Home: Your child took a pretest on adding -s and -es to nouns. **Home Activity:** Help your child learn misspelled words before the final test. Your child should look at the word, say it, spell it aloud, and then spell it with eyes shut.

Spelling: Adding -s and -es

Think and Practice

Word List

months	valleys	pictures	benches	dresses
friends	donkeys	mornings	speeches	batteries
grades	missiles	matches	passes	companies
cowboys	costumes	bushes	kisses	centuries

Directions: Write the word from the box that is formed by adding **-es** to each base word. Hint: In some cases, you need to change the **y** to **i** before adding **-es**.

1. match _____
2. bench _____
3. kiss _____
4. dress _____
5. speech _____

6. pass _____
7. bush _____
8. century _____
9. company _____
10. battery _____

Directions: Choose the word from the box that is formed by adding **-s** to each base word. Write the letters of the word on the blanks. The boxed letters spell something you do to form plurals.

11. valley
12. grade
13. donkey
14. cowboy
15. month
16. friend
17. costume
18. morning
19. picture
20. missile

11. __ ☐ __ __ __ __ __
12. __ __ __ ☐ __ __
13. __ __ ☐ __ __ __ __ __
14. __ __ ☐ __ __ __ __
15. __ __ ☐ __ __ __
16. __ __ __ __ __ ☐
17. __ ☐ __ __ __ __ __
18. __ __ ☐ __ __ __ __
19. __ __ __ __ __ ☐ __
20. __ __ ☐ __ __

Something you do to form plurals: __ __ __ __ __ __ __ __ __ __ __

Notes for Home: Your child spelled words that have *-s* and *-es* added to them to form plurals. *Home Activity:* Pick out items from the room whose names your child can spell. Then have your child spell the plural by adding *-s* or *-es*.

Spelling: Adding -s and -es

Directions: Proofread this letter. Find five spelling mistakes. Use the proofreading marks to correct each mistake.

☰	Make a capital.
╱	Make a small letter.
∧	Add something.
ℐ	Take out something.
⊙	Add a period.
¶	Begin a new paragraph.

Dear Jenna,

   It's been two monthes since we moved here after Dad switched companys. I've made some new friends, and my grades are okay. I got two new dresess and hung new picturs on my wall. However, some mornings I wish I were back in my old home.

                    Hugs and kissess,

                    Tina

Word List

months	donkeys	matches	kisses
friends	missiles	bushes	dresses
grades	costumes	benches	batteries
cowboys	pictures	speeches	companies
valleys	mornings	passes	centuries

Write a Friendly Letter

Imagine you are Tina's friend Jenna. On a separate sheet of paper, write a friendly letter that tells what it is like when your best friend moves away. Try to use at least five of your spelling words.

Spelling Tip

Adding -es

Add **-es** to words that end in **sh, ch, s, ss,** or **x.** If the word ends in **consonant** and **y**, change y to **i** before adding **-es.**

Notes for Home: Your child spelled words that have -*s* and -*es* added to them to form plurals. *Home Activity:* Say each spelling word aloud, leaving off the final sound /s/. For example, say *picture,* not *pictures.* Have your child spell the plural form of the word.

Name _____

Spelling: Adding -s and -es

REVIEW

Word List				
months	valleys	pictures	benches	dresses
friends	donkeys	mornings	speeches	batteries
grades	missiles	matches	passes	companies
cowboys	costumes	bushes	kisses	centuries

Directions: Choose the word from the box that best completes each sentence.
Write the word on the line to the left.

_____ 1. Our _____ next door are leaving the neighborhood.

_____ 2. They've been planning to move for _____.

_____ 3. They've been waking early in the _____ to pack.

_____ 4. One of the moving _____ sent its van over today.

_____ 5. We stood near the rose _____ and watched the movers.

_____ 6. They carried out _____ that once hung on the walls.

_____ 7. They took girls' _____ that had hung in a closet.

_____ 8. They took wooden _____ from the backyard.

_____ 9. Some neighbors praised the family in brief _____.

_____ 10. After hugs and _____, the family drove away.

Directions: Write the word from the box that matches each clue.

_____ 11. sky rockets

_____ 12. similar to mules

_____ 13. actors' outfits

_____ 14. candle lighters

_____ 15. A and B+, for example

_____ 16. horse riders

_____ 17. hundreds of years

_____ 18. between hills

_____ 19. used in flashlights

_____ 20. thrown in football

Notes for Home: Your child spelled words that have -s and -es added to them to form plurals.
Home Activity: Spell a word that names one thing, such as *table* or *glass*. See if your child
can spell the plural by adding -s or -es.

Spelling: Irregular Plurals

Pretest Directions: Fold back the page along the dotted line. On the blanks, write the spelling words as they are dictated. When you have finished the test, unfold the page and check your words.

1._____

2._____

3._____

4._____

5._____

6._____

7._____

8._____

9._____

10._____

11._____

12._____

13._____

14._____

15._____

16._____

17._____

18._____

19._____

20._____

1. Some **radios** run on batteries.

2. The store rents **videos**.

3. **Pianos** are very heavy.

4. Some houses have **patios**.

5. Bluegrass music uses **banjos**.

6. This book has stories of **heroes**.

7. Baked **potatoes** are tasty.

8. The cave is full of **echoes**.

9. **Tornadoes** cause damage.

10. These **tomatoes** are not ripe yet

11. The **cuffs** of his pants are dirty.

12. **Cliffs** rise high above the river.

13. We have the same **beliefs**.

14. Animal **hoofs** are hard.

15. All the **roofs** were full of snow.

16. They talked among **themselves**.

17. Paramedics save **lives**.

18. The **leaves** are turning red.

19. These **loaves** of bread are stale.

20. They cut the fruit into **halves**.

Notes for Home: Your child took a pretest on words that are irregular plurals. *Home Activity:* Help your child learn misspelled words before the final test. Your child can underline the word parts that caused the problems and concentrate on those parts.

Spelling: Irregular Plurals

Think and Practice

Word List				
radios	banjos	tornadoes	beliefs	lives
videos	heroes	tomatoes	hoofs	leaves
pianos	potatoes	cuffs	roofs	loaves
patios	echoes	cliffs	themselves	halves

Directions: Choose the words from the box that are formed by adding **-es** to a base word. Write each word in the correct column.

f changes to v before -es is added

1. _____
2. _____
3. _____
4. _____
5. _____

-es is added to words ending with o

6. _____
7. _____
8. _____
9. _____
10. _____

Directions: Add **-s** to each word in ( ) to form a word from the box and complete the sentence. Write the word on the line.

_____ 11. The horses' (hoof) loosened several rocks.

_____ 12. Rocks from the (cliff) fell onto the land below.

_____ 13. Some rocks went through the (roof) of old buildings.

_____ 14. Other rocks crashed onto several (patio).

_____ 15. A rescue alert was heard on many (radio).

_____ 16. All differing customs and (belief) were set aside during the rescue.

_____ 17. One musician was able to rescue her two (piano).

_____ 18. But she wasn't able to save her damaged (banjo).

_____ 19. One man escaped with only minor tears to his shirt (cuff).

_____ 20. Newscasts showed home (video) of the damage shot by the homeowners.

Notes for Home: Your child spelled irregular plural nouns that have *-s* and *-es* added to them but that do not follow regular spelling patterns. *Home Activity:* Spell each spelling word aloud to your child. Have your child spell each word you say.

Spelling: Irregular Plurals

Directions: Proofread this news bulletin. Find five spelling mistakes. Use the proofreading marks to correct each mistake.

Proofread and Write

Proofreading Marks	
≡	Make a capital.
/	Make a small letter.
∧	Add something.
✄	Take out something.
⊙	Add a period.
¶	Begin a new paragraph.

News Bulletin!

Alert! Several tornados have been spotted near the cliffs. The rooves of some homes have been damaged. No lifes have been lost, and many have been rescued. People should shut themselfs safely in their basements and stay off their patios. Do not try to take home videoes. Stay tuned to your radios for updated reports.

Word List

radios	banjos	tornadoes	beliefs	lives
videos	heroes	tomatoes	hoofs	leaves
pianos	potatoes	cuffs	roofs	loaves
patios	echoes	cliffs	themselves	halves

Write a News Report

Imagine you are a news correspondent reporting the results of a storm. On a separate sheet of paper, write your news report. Try to use at least five of your spelling words.

Spelling Tip

potatoes

How can you remember to spell **potatoes,** not **potatos?** Think of this hint: **Pota<u>toes</u>** have both eyes and <u>toes</u>.

Notes for Home: Your child spelled irregular plural nouns that have -*s* and -*es* added to them but that do not follow regular spelling patterns. *Home Activity:* Make a list of the spelling words, but misspell several words. Have your child correct the list.

Spelling: Irregular Plurals

REVIEW

Word List				
radios	banjos	tornadoes	beliefs	lives
videos	heroes	tomatoes	hoofs	leaves
pianos	potatoes	cuffs	roofs	loaves
patios	echoes	cliffs	themselves	halves

Directions: Choose the word from the box that best completes each statement. Write the word on the line to the left.

_____ 1. *Strings* are to *violins* as *keys* are to ____.

_____ 2. *People* are to *feet* as *horses* are to ____.

_____ 3. *Below* is to *basements* as *above* is to ____.

_____ 4. *Corn* is to *ears* as *bread* is to ____.

_____ 5. *Talent* is to *artists* as *bravery* is to ____.

_____ 6. *Head* is to *hair* as *tree* is to ____.

_____ 7. *We* is to *ourselves* as *they* is to ____.

_____ 8. *Green* is to *lettuce* as *red* is to ____.

_____ 9. *Shake* is to *earthquakes* as *swirl* is to ____.

_____ 10. *Bang* is to *drums* as *strum* is to ____.

_____ 11. *Creamed* is to *spinach* as *mashed* is to ____.

_____ 12. *Arms* is to *hands* as *sleeves* is to ____.

Directions: Choose the word from the box that answers each question. Write the word on the line.

_____ 13. What might you rent for a double feature?

_____ 14. Where would you not want to walk if you were afraid of heights?

_____ 15. What might you hear when you shout in the Grand Canyon?

_____ 16. What would you learn about if you read biographies?

_____ 17. Where do people hold barbecues in the summer?

_____ 18. What do teenagers usually play too loud?

_____ 19. Into what would you cut a pie for two very big eaters?

_____ 20. What do you call strong feelings or ideas?

Notes for Home: Your child spelled irregular plural nouns that have *-s* and *-es* added to them but that do not follow regular spelling patterns. **Home Activity:** Give your child clues about each spelling word. See if your child can identify and spell each word.

© Scott Foresman 5

Spelling: Contractions

Pretest Directions: Fold back the page along the dotted line. On the blanks, write the spelling words as they are dictated. When you have finished the test, unfold the page and check your words.

1._____
2._____
3._____
4._____
5._____
6._____
7._____
8._____
9._____
10._____
11._____
12._____
13._____
14._____
15._____
16._____
17._____
18._____
19._____
20._____

1. Carrie **can't** sing very well.
2. I **wouldn't** know.
3. **Don't** you live nearby?
4. They **weren't** happy with him.
5. **I'm** writing a letter to a friend.
6. **I'll** tell you about it later.
7. **Let's** go to the movies tonight.
8. **That's** not what I meant.
9. **There's** someone at the door.
10. **What's** your favorite color?
11. **She's** trying to pay attention.
12. **You're** not crying, are you?
13. **They're** waiting for a ride home.
14. **Who's** coming to the party?
15. **We're** having a picnic tomorrow.
16. **I've** finished reading my book.
17. **You've** helped me a lot.
18. We **should've** taken the bus.
19. Tammy **could've** fixed anything.
20. **We've** only just arrived.

Notes for Home: Your child took a pretest on words that are contractions. *Home Activity:* Help your child learn misspelled words. Dictate the word and have your child spell the word aloud for you or write it on paper, making sure the apostrophe is in the correct place.

Think and Practice

Spelling: Contractions

Word List			
can't	I'll	she's	I've
wouldn't	let's	you're	you've
don't	that's	they're	should've
weren't	there's	who's	could've
I'm	what's	we're	we've

Directions: Choose the words from the box that contain the pronouns **I, you, she, we, they,** and **us.** Write the words in alphabetical order.

1. _____   6. _____

2. _____   7. _____

3. _____   8. _____

4. _____   9. _____

5. _____   10. _____

Directions: Write the word from the box that matches each clue.

_____ **11.** It rhymes with *could've* and means "should have."

_____ **12.** It rhymes with *burnt* and means "were not."

_____ **13.** It rhymes with *won't* and means "do not."

_____ **14.** It rhymes with *bats* and means "that is."

_____ **15.** It rhymes with *cuts* and means "what is."

_____ **16.** It rhymes with *shoes* and means "who is."

_____ **17.** It rhymes with *should've* and means "could have."

_____ **18.** It rhymes with *shouldn't* and means "would not."

_____ **19.** It rhymes with *bears* and means "there is."

_____ **20.** It rhymes with *ant* and means "cannot."

Notes for Home: Your child spelled contractions. *Home Activity:* Read a story with your child. Have your child identify the contractions and explain which two words have been combined to form each contraction.

50   Spelling: Contractions

Spelling: Contractions

Directions: Proofread this speech. Find five spelling mistakes. Use the proofreading marks to correct each mistake.

Proofread and Write

≡ Make a capital.
／ Make a small letter.
∧ Add something.
✍ Take out something.
⊙ Add a period.
⊬ Begin a new paragraph.

> As team captain, I'm telling you players that wev'e got to practice more if we're going to win games. We shouldv'e won yesterday, and we could've won. But we're making too many mistakes, and thats' hurting us. We ca'nt win if we don't practice. So let's work hard and show whose the best!

Word List

can't	I'll	she's	I've
wouldn't	let's	you're	you've
don't	that's	they're	should've
weren't	there's	who's	could've
I'm	what's	we're	we've

Write a Pep Talk

Imagine you were coach of the team addressed above. On a separate sheet of paper, write a pep talk to give to team members. Try to use at least five of your spelling words.

Spelling Tip

who's

Don't confuse **who's** with **whose**. Use **who's** when it takes the place of the words **who is.**

Notes for Home: Your child spelled contractions—words made of two other words with an apostrophe representing the missing letters. **Home Activity:** Say the two words that each spelling word combines, such as *let us* for *let's*. Have your child spell the contraction.

Spelling: Contractions

Word List			
can't	I'll	she's	I've
wouldn't	let's	you're	you've
don't	that's	they're	should've
weren't	there's	who's	could've
I'm	what's	we're	we've

Directions: Choose the word from the box that can replace the underlined words in each sentence. Write the word on the line to the left.

_____ **1.** I hear <u>there is</u> band practice today.

_____ **2.** I <u>do not</u> know the exact time, however.

_____ **3.** I think <u>we are</u> practicing right after school.

_____ **4.** <u>I will</u> check the exact time.

_____ **5.** Do you know where <u>they are</u> holding it?

_____ **6.** <u>I am</u> pretty sure it is on the football field.

_____ **7.** They <u>should have</u> told us already.

_____ **8.** Do you know <u>who is</u> leading the practice?

_____ **9.** Ms. Davis told me that <u>she is</u> attending.

_____ **10.** However, she <u>would not</u> say if she is leading it.

_____ **11.** <u>I have</u> got to be home by six o'clock.

_____ **12.** <u>Let us</u> hope that practice is over by then.

Directions: Choose the word from the box that means the same as each word or words below. Write the word on the lines.

13. could have _____

14. what is_____

15. cannot _____

16. we have _____

17. you are_____

18. were not _____

19. you have _____

20. that is _____

Notes for Home: Your child spelled contractions—words made of two other words with an apostrophe representing the missing letters. **Home Activity:** Spell each spelling word aloud, without saying "apostrophe." See if your child can tell you where the apostrophe (') belongs.

Spelling: Capitalization

Pretest Directions: Fold back the page along the dotted line. On the blanks, write the spelling words as they are dictated. When you have finished the test, unfold the page and check your words.

1._____

2._____

3._____

4._____

5._____

6._____

7._____

8._____

9._____

10._____

11._____

12._____

13._____

14._____

15._____

16._____

17._____

18._____

19._____

20._____

1. Her sister went to **Houston**.

2. It gets very cold in **Alaska**.

3. I have never been to **Kentucky**.

4. We are going to **Little Rock**.

5. Where is **Duluth** on the map?

6. Much of **Arizona** is desert.

7. **Miami** is in Florida.

8. Hoosiers are from **Indiana**.

9. **Alabama** is in the south.

10. I live in **South Carolina**.

11. Have you been to **Baltimore**?

12. Cars are made in **Detroit**.

13. **Los Angeles** is near the ocean.

14. **Hawaii** is made up of islands.

15. I want to go back to **Memphis**.

16. Jefferson lived in **Virginia**.

17. Eugene is a city in **Oregon**.

18. **Pittsburgh** is my hometown.

19. **Texas** is a large state.

20. It is warm in **Florida**.

Notes for Home: Your child took a pretest on capitalized words. *Home Activity:* Help your child learn misspelled words before the final test. Have your child divide misspelled words into parts (such as syllables) and concentrate on each part.

Spelling: Capitalization

Think and Practice

Word List				
Houston	Duluth	Alabama	Los Angeles	Oregon
Alaska	Arizona	South Carolina	Hawaii	Pittsburgh
Kentucky	Miami	Baltimore	Memphis	Texas
Little Rock	Indiana	Detroit	Virginia	Florida

Directions: Choose the words from the box that name U.S. states. Write the words in alphabetical order.

1. _____   7. _____

2. _____   8. _____

3. _____   9. _____

4. _____   10. _____

5. _____   11. _____

6. _____

Directions: Choose the word from the box that answers each question. Write the word on the line.

_____ 12. Which city has the word *angel* in it?

_____ 13. Which city has the word *his* in it?

_____ 14. Which city has the word *pit* in it?

_____ 15. Which city rhymes with *truth?*

_____ 16. Which city has *us* in the middle?

_____ 17. Which city means the same as *pebble?*

_____ 18. Which city rhymes with *exploit?*

_____ 19. Which city has the word *more* in it?

_____ 20. Which city has the word *am* in the middle?

Notes for Home: Your child spelled names of cities and states. *Home Activity:* Look at a map of the United States with your child. Together, try to find all the states and cities that are spelling words. Have your child identify the capital letter or letters in each name.

Spelling: Capitalization

Directions: Proofread this article. Find five spelling mistakes. Use the proofreading marks to correct each mistake.

≡	Make a capital.
/	Make a small letter.
∧	Add something.
✰	Take out something.
⊙	Add a period.
¶	Begin a new paragraph.

Many cities and states are famous for their products. In detriot, many people make cars. In Florida, thousands work on citrus farms. Lots of farmers have cotton fields in Alabama and South carolina, while others have tobacco fields in virgina. Oregon has lumberjacks, huseton has oil workers, and pitsburgh has many steel workers.

Spelling Tip
Hawaii
The end of the word **Hawaii** can be tricky to spell. Remember this hint: See **Hawaii** with your two eyes **(ii)**.

Word List

Houston	Duluth	Alabama	Los Angeles	Oregon
Alaska	Arizona	South Carolina	Hawaii	Pittsburgh
Kentucky	Miami	Baltimore	Memphis	Texas
Little Rock	Indiana	Detroit	Virginia	Florida

Write a Report

Find out more about the different states and cities listed in the box. On a separate sheet of paper, write a report with your information. Try to use at least five cities or states.

Notes for Home: Your child spelled names of cities and states. *Home Activity:* Begin to spell each spelling word slowly, one letter at a time. When your child recognizes the word, have him or her complete its spelling.

Spelling: Capitalization

REVIEW

Word List

Houston	Duluth	Alabama	Los Angeles	Oregon
Alaska	Arizona	South Carolina	Hawaii	Pittsburgh
Kentucky	Miami	Baltimore	Memphis	Texas
Little Rock	Indiana	Detroit	Virginia	Florida

Directions: Choose the word from the box that best matches each clue. Use a map of the United States to help you. Write the word on the line.

_____ 1. This state is between Canada and Russia.

_____ 2. This state is south of Oklahoma.

_____ 3. This state is south of Utah.

_____ 4. This state is between Ohio and Illinois.

_____ 5. This state is east of West Virginia.

_____ 6. This state is just north of Tennessee.

_____ 7. This state is between Mississippi and Georgia.

_____ 8. This state is just south of North Carolina.

_____ 9. This state is actually a group of islands.

_____ 10. This state is south of Washington state.

_____ 11. This state is south of Georgia.

Directions: Choose the word from the box that names a city located in each state below. Use a map of the United States to help you. Write the word on the line.

_____ 12. Tennessee

_____ 13. Arkansas

_____ 14. Pennsylvania

_____ 15. Texas

_____ 16. Michigan

_____ 17. Florida

_____ 18. California

_____ 19. Minnesota

_____ 20. Maryland

Notes for Home: Your child spelled names of cities and states. **Home Activity:** Say each spelling word aloud. See if your child can locate the state or city on a map of the United States. Then have your child close his or her eyes and spell the word.

Spelling: Possessives

Pretest Directions: Fold back the page along the dotted line. On the blanks, write the spelling words as they are dictated. When you have finished the test, unfold the page and check your words.

1._____

2._____

3._____

4._____

5._____

6._____

7._____

8._____

9._____

10._____

11._____

12._____

13._____

14._____

15._____

16._____

17._____

18._____

19._____

20._____

1. These are my **friend's** toys.

2. Has **today's** mail arrived yet?

3. **Dad's** magazine came today.

4. **Mom's** books are on the shelf.

5. My little **sister's** doll was broken.

6. My **sisters'** dresses are blue.

7. That **child's** face needs washing.

8. The **children's** drawings are here.

9. Did you see that **person's** hat?

10. **People's** intentions are good.

11. My **grandmother's** cat is sick.

12. Her **grandfather's** car is outside.

13. Our **uncle's** name is Steven.

14. Their **uncles'** homes are old.

15. The **doctor's** coat is white.

16. That is the **doctors'** entrance.

17. My **cousin's** hair is red.

18. Their **cousins'** names are long.

19. That **woman's** coat is brown.

20. That store sells **women's** clothes.

Notes for Home: Your child took a pretest on words that show ownership, or possessives. *Home Activity:* Help your child learn misspelled words before the final test, concentrating on whether one person or more than one person owns something.

Spelling: Possessives

Think and Practice

Word List			
friend's	sisters'	grandmother's	doctors'
today's	child's	grandfather's	cousin's
Dad's	children's	uncle's	cousins'
Mom's	person's	uncles'	woman's
sister's	people's	doctor's	women's

Directions: Choose the words from the box that name ownership by one person or thing. Write the words on the lines.

1. _____   8. _____

2. _____   9. _____

3. _____   10. _____

4. _____   11. _____

5. _____   12. _____

6. _____   13. _____

7. _____

Directions: Choose the word from the box to complete each equation, using a plural possessive noun. Write your word on the line.

_____ **14.** the pets of the children = the _____ pets

_____ **15.** the offices of the doctors = the _____ offices

_____ **16.** the jobs of the people = the _____ jobs

_____ **17.** the farm of the cousins = the _____ farm

_____ **18.** the ducks of the uncles = the _____ ducks

_____ **19.** the votes of the women = the _____ votes

_____ **20.** the hogs of the sisters = the _____ hogs

Notes for Home: Your child spelled possessive nouns—words that show ownership. *Home Activity:* Look at magazine pictures together. Invite your child to identify people and their possessions, such as *the farmer's hat,* and spell each possessive noun.

Spelling: Possessives

Directions: Proofread this diary entry. Find five spelling mistakes.
Use the proofreading marks to correct each mistake.

≡	Make a capital.
/	Make a small letter.
∧	Add something.
✎	Take out something.
⊙	Add a period.
¶	Begin a new paragraph.

Dear Diary,

Today's trip to our uncle's farm was fun! I rode my
grandmothers horse. Later, it was my two cousin's
turns. The horse licked my one cousin's face! Later we
took a childrens' tour of the farm. I saw Moms' favorite
duck and Dad's favorite pig. My grandfather's favorite
is the old hen who lays an egg every day. I think farm
animals' lives are better than peoples' lives!

Spelling Tip

sister's   sisters'

To form possessives of singular nouns,
add an **apostrophe (')** and **s: sister's.**
For plural nouns that end in **-s**, add an
apostrophe ('): sisters'. For plural
nouns that do not end in **-s**, add
apostrophe (') and **s: children's.**

Word List

friend's	grandmother's
today's	grandfather's
Dad's	uncle's
Mom's	uncles'
sister's	doctor's
sisters'	doctors'
child's	cousin's
children's	cousins'
person's	woman's
people's	women's

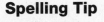

Write a Diary Entry

Imagine you are a farm animal who keeps a diary. On a separate sheet of paper,
write a diary entry that describes a typical day on the farm. Try to use at least
five of your spelling words.

Notes for Home: Your child spelled possessive nouns—words that show ownership. **Home
Activity:** Have your child make a list of items or places around the house, using possessive
nouns. For example: *Mom's favorite chair* or *my twin sisters' room.*

Spelling: Possessives

Word List

friend's	sister's	person's	uncle's	cousin's
today's	sisters'	people's	uncles'	cousins'
Dad's	child's	grandmother's	doctor's	woman's
Mom's	children's	grandfather's	doctors'	women's

Directions: Choose the word from the box that is the possessive form of the underlined word in each sentence. Write the possessive noun on the line.

_____ 1. The vacation of the <u>children</u> was spent on a farm.

_____ 2. They visited the farm of the <u>cousins</u> in Iowa.

_____ 3. On the farm, the work of a <u>person</u> is important.

_____ 4. The job of the <u>grandmother</u> is to feed the chicks.

_____ 5. The job of the <u>uncles</u> is to milk the cows.

_____ 6. The job of the <u>women</u> is to collect chicken eggs.

_____ 7. The job of one <u>child</u> is to feed hay to the horses.

_____ 8. The suggestion of <u>Mom</u> was to help out with chores.

_____ 9. Shearing the sheep was one chore of <u>today</u>.

_____ 10. The children assisted with the help of <u>Dad</u>.

_____ 11. The task of the <u>sister</u> was to gather the wool.

_____ 12. Later the animals received an exam of a <u>doctor</u>.

Directions: Choose the word from the box that is the possessive form of each word below. Write the word on the line.

13. friend _____   **17.** sisters _____

14. cousin _____   **18.** doctors _____

15. grandfather _____   **19.** uncle _____

16. people _____   **20.** woman _____

Notes for Home: Your child spelled possessive nouns—words that show ownership. ***Home Activity:*** Read a magazine article with your child. Together, identify possessive nouns that you find. Have your child tell whether each noun is singular or plural.

Spelling: Homophones

Pretest Directions: Fold back the page along the dotted line. On the blanks, write the spelling words as they are dictated. When you have finished the test, unfold the page and check your words.

1. _____
2. _____
3. _____
4. _____
5. _____
6. _____
7. _____
8. _____
9. _____
10. _____
11. _____
12. _____
13. _____
14. _____
15. _____
16. _____
17. _____
18. _____
19. _____
20. _____

1. Please **write** to me.
2. You must do what is **right**.
3. Ted wants to **buy** a candy bar.
4. The book is **by** a famous author.
5. This letter is **to** your mother.
6. There are **too** many choices.
7. Are you **bored** by this movie?
8. I need some nails and a **board**.
9. **It's** easy to ride a bike.
10. The bird spread **its** wings.
11. Jason **threw** the baseball to me.
12. The kids ran **through** the yard.
13. You must **knead** the dough.
14. I **need** to see you tomorrow.
15. This is the library's **main** branch.
16. The lion shook his **mane**.
17. I forget things about the **past**.
18. The truck **passed** the school bus.
19. Are you **allowed** to go?
20. She was reading **aloud**.

Notes for Home: Your child took a pretest on homophones, words that sound alike but are spelled differently and have different meanings. *Home Activity:* Help your child learn to connect the spelling of the word with its meaning.

Spelling: Homophones

Word List				
write	to	it's	knead	past
right	too	its	need	passed
buy	bored	threw	main	allowed
by	board	through	mane	aloud

Directions: Read each sentence. Then match each underlined word to its definition. Write the word on the line.

He <u>threw</u> the ball <u>through</u> the window.

    tossed   from end to end

1. _____   2. _____

You <u>need</u> to <u>knead</u> the dough to make bread.

    must   press together

5. _____   6. _____

Are you going <u>to</u> the ball game <u>too</u>?

    also   in the direction of

3. _____   4. _____

We <u>buy</u> our milk <u>by</u> the gallon.

    in the amount of   purchase

7. _____   8. _____

Directions: Choose the word from the box that best completes each sentence. Write the word on the line to the left.

_____ 9. Did you _____ the thank-you letter?

_____ 10. Please do it _____ now.

_____ 11. The lions were the _____ circus attraction,

_____ 12. The biggest lion had a magnificent _____.

_____ 13. The _____ meeting went on for hours.

_____ 14. I was so _____ I nearly fell asleep.

_____ 15. Father _____ the potatoes to me.

_____ 16. We finished eating at half _____ four.

_____ 17. I think _____ time for dessert.

_____ 18. I gave the dog a piece of cake in _____ bowl.

_____ 19. You're not _____ to talk loudly in the library.

_____ 20. You also can't read _____ in the library.

Notes for Home: Your child spelled homophones—words that sound the same but have different spellings and meanings. *Home Activity:* Make up short sentences using one spelling word in each sentence. Say each sentence and have your child spell the word you used.

Spelling: Homophones

Directions: Proofread the rules for how to behave at a special dinner. Find seven spelling mistakes. Use the proofreading marks to correct each mistake.

≡	Make a capital.
/	Make a small letter.
∧	Add something.
ℐ	Take out something.
⊙	Add a period.
¶	Begin a new paragraph.

Always place your napkin in your lap before eating.

Hold the fork in your left hand, and the knife in your write.

If you need to have a dish past, always ask politely.

Never sing or read allowed at the table, unless asked too do so.

Avoid yawning, even if you are bord.

When you are thru eating, wait for others to finish before

leaving the table.

Remember to thank your host buy the time you leave.

Spelling Tip

it's   its

Homophones are words that sound alike but have different spellings and meanings. Don't confuse the homophones **its** and **it's**. **It's** means **it is**. **Its** is a possessive pronoun that means **belonging to it.** Remember: **It's** easy to remember **its** spelling: **i-t.**

Word List

write	threw
right	through
buy	knead
by	need
to	main
too	mane
bored	past
board	passed
it's	allowed
its	aloud

Write a Set of Rules

On a separate sheet of paper, write your own rules for another social situation, such as talking on the telephone or meeting new people. Try to use at least five of your spelling words.

Notes for Home: Your child spelled homophones—words that sound exactly alike but have different spellings and meanings. *Home Activity:* Write each pair of homophones on index cards. Take turns choosing a card and writing a sentence that uses both words.

Spelling: Homophones

Word List				
write	to	it's	knead	past
right	too	its	need	passed
buy	bored	threw	main	allowed
by	board	through	mane	aloud

Directions: Choose the word from the box that has the same or nearly the same meaning as each word or words below. Write the word on the line.

1. wooden plank _____

2. finished _____

3. purchase _____

4. uninterested _____

5. most important _____

6. squeeze _____

7. hair _____

8. near _____

9. require _____

10. pitched _____

Directions: Choose a pair of homophones from the box to complete each sentence. Write the words on the lines to the left.

_____ 11. It's _____ late _____ go to the parade.

_____ 12.

_____ 13. We _____ the marchers when we drove _____ the bank.

_____ 14.

_____ 15. I should _____ myself a note _____ now before I forget.

_____ 16.

_____ 17. When the cat meows, _____ time for _____ dinner.

_____ 18.

_____ 19. The teacher _____ the students to read _____ to one another.

_____ 20.

Notes for Home: Your child spelled homophones—words that sound alike but are spelled differently and have different meanings. *Home Activity:* Help your child write a short rhyming poem using several of the spelling words.

Spelling: Including All the Letters

Pretest Directions: Fold back the page along the dotted line. On the blanks, write the spelling words as they are dictated. When you have finished the test, unfold the page and check your words.

1._____

2._____

3._____

4._____

5._____

6._____

7._____

8._____

9._____

10._____

11._____

12._____

13._____

14._____

15._____

16._____

17._____

18._____

19._____

20._____

1. What is the **answer**?

2. Sixty seconds make a **minute**.

3. Something **happened** today.

4. Let's go to the **library**.

5. The store **opened** last week.

6. What is the **length** of the track?

7. I am **getting** a dog.

8. We leave **when** the bell rings.

9. I have **finished** my work.

10. **Maybe** they will come tomorrow.

11. His mom likes **mystery** novels.

12. It is time to go to the **dentist**.

13. I am not **actually** afraid.

14. The car is five feet in **width**.

15. My sundae has **caramel** topping.

16. Please pass the **pumpkin** pie.

17. I found a **quarter** on the stairs.

18. I ate a roast beef **sandwich**.

19. The monkey **grabbed** the banana.

20. Thunder can be **frightening**.

Notes for Home: Your child took a pretest on words that have difficult letter combinations. *Home Activity:* Help your child learn misspelled words before the final test. Your child can underline the word parts that caused the problems and concentrate on those parts.

Spelling: Including All the Letters

Word List				
answer	opened	finished	actually	quarter
minute	length	maybe	width	sandwich
happened	getting	mystery	caramel	grabbed
library	when	dentist	pumpkin	frightening

Directions: Choose the word from the box that is formed by adding an ending to each base word. Write the word on the line.

1. open _____

2. actual _____

3. happen _____

4. frighten _____

5. get _____

6. grab _____

7. finish _____

Directions: Choose the word from the box that best matches each definition. Write the word on the line.

_____ **8.** It's a fall vegetable.

_____ **9.** It's a home for books.

_____ **10.** It's a popular luncheon food made with bread.

_____ **11.** It means the same as "perhaps."

_____ **12.** It's the same as sixty seconds.

_____ **13.** It's a sticky candy you put on apples.

_____ **14.** It's the distance you measure from end to end.

_____ **15.** It's a reply.

_____ **16.** It's the distance across.

_____ **17.** It's a tooth doctor.

_____ **18.** It's something that is hard to figure out, like a puzzle.

_____ **19.** It's a word you use to ask about the time something begins.

_____ **20.** It's the same as one-fourth.

Notes for Home: Your child spelled words that have more letters than one might expect. *Home Activity:* Have a spelling bee with your child, taking turns spelling the words from the box. If one of you spells a word incorrectly, the other must try to spell it correctly.

Spelling: Including All the Letters

Directions: Proofread the letter. Find five spelling mistakes. Use the proofreading marks to correct each mistake.

≡	Make a capital.
/	Make a small letter.
∧	Add something.
ℐ	Take out something.
⊙	Add a period.
¶	Begin a new paragraph.

Dear Paul,

When I opend your letter, I had just finushed feeding our new husky puppy. Then I saw the picture of your new puppy! Isn't it cool? We both have huskies! I got some books out of the libary about dogsled racing. It acually sounds like a really fun sport. Maybe some day we'll compete in the Iditarod. Write back and tell me how your dog is geting along.

Love,

Keiko

Spelling Tip

Some words have more letters than you might think. When spelling these words, pronounce each syllable carefully. You'll be less likely to leave out letters.

Word List

answer
minute
happened
library
opened
length
getting
when
finished
maybe
mystery
dentist
actually
width
caramel
pumpkin
quarter
sandwich
grabbed
frightening

Write a Letter

On a separate sheet of paper, write a letter that Paul might send back to Keiko. Try to use at least five of your spelling words.

Notes for Home: Your child spelled words that have more letters than one might expect.
Home Activity: On a piece of paper, write the spelling words with the letters scrambled. Invite your child to unscramble the letters to spell each word.

Spelling: Including All the Letters   REVIEW

Word List				
answer	opened	finished	actually	quarter
minute	length	maybe	width	sandwich
happened	getting	mystery	caramel	grabbed
library	when	dentist	pumpkin	frightening

Directions: Write the word from the box that belongs in each group of words.

1. distance, long measure, _____

2. squash, gourd, _____

3. second, hour, _____

4. doctor, veterinarian, _____

5. soup, salad, _____

6. gym, cafeteria, _____

7. nickel, dime, _____

8. folk tale, science fiction, _____

9. fudge, butterscotch, _____

10. wideness, measure side to side, _____

Directions: Choose the word from the box that best completes each sentence in the paragraph. Write the word on the matching numbered lines to the right.

My Most Embarrassing Moment

It was my first dogsled race and I was **11.** _____ quite nervous. Then, **12.** _____ the race began, I **13.** _____ the reins and told my dogs to "Mush!" The dogs' **14.** _____ was to bark and take off. Then it **15.** _____. A bag of supplies somehow **16.** _____ and everything spilled out. I pulled hard on the reins, **17.** _____ a bit too hard. It was **18.** _____ how fast the sled flipped over. As I was **19.** _____ up, I saw four other sleds pass us. I knew then I'd be lucky if I **20.** _____ the race at all!

11. _____
12. _____
13. _____
14. _____
15. _____
16. _____
17. _____
18. _____
19. _____
20. _____

Notes for Home: Your child spelled words that have more letters than might be expected. *Home Activity:* Challenge your child to pronounce each spelling word carefully and then spell it. Talk about how sounding out each syllable makes it easier to spell these words.

Name_____

Spelling: Adding -ed and -ing, -er and -est

Pretest Directions: Fold back the page along the dotted line. On the blanks, write the spelling words as they are dictated. When you have finished the test, unfold the page and check your words.

1._____

2._____

3._____

4._____

5._____

6._____

7._____

8._____

9._____

10._____

11._____

12._____

13._____

14._____

15._____

16._____

17._____

18._____

19._____

20._____

1. We **followed** the rules.

2. The chicks are **following** the hen.

3. This bag is **lighter** than the other.

4. You can carry the **lightest** box.

5. He **tried** to remain quiet.

6. I am **trying** to remember her.

7. Which of the two cats is **cuter**?

8. My neighbor had the **cutest** baby.

9. The children were very **excited**.

10. Fireworks can be **exciting**.

11. The teacher was **amused**.

12. The joke was very **amusing**.

13. Melons are **bigger** than oranges.

14. Sequoias are the **biggest** trees.

15. Are the presents all **wrapped**?

16. We need more **wrapping** paper.

17. We should have left **earlier**.

18. I need to catch the **earliest** flight.

19. Is math **easier** than science?

20. Do not give me the **easiest** job.

Notes for Home: Your child took a pretest on adding *-ed, -ing, -er,* and *-est* to words. ***Home Activity:*** Help your child learn misspelled words before the final test. Dictate the word and have your child spell the word aloud for you or write it on paper.

Spelling: Adding -ed and -ing, -er and -est

Word List				
followed	tried	excited	bigger	earlier
following	trying	exciting	biggest	earliest
lighter	cuter	amused	wrapped	easier
lightest	cutest	amusing	wrapping	easiest

Directions: Choose the word from the box that is formed by adding **-er** or **-est** to each base word. Write the word on the correct line.

Base Word	Add -er	Add -est
big	1. _____	2. _____
cute	3. _____	4. _____
early	5. _____	6. _____
light	7. _____	8. _____
easy	9. _____	10. _____

Directions: Add **-ed** or **-ing** to the word in ( ) to form a word from the box and to complete each sentence. Write the word on the line.

_____ 11. Sarah is not very (excite) about tonight's sleepover.

_____ 12. She (try) spending the night at a friend's once before.

_____ 13. She started out thinking it was (excite) to be there.

_____ 14. An hour after the lights went out, Sarah was still (try) to sleep.

_____ 15. She (amuse) herself by counting the teddy bears on the wallpaper.

_____ 16. She started (follow) the teddy bears in her imagination.

_____ 17. She (wrap) herself tightly in her sleeping bag.

_____ 18. She (follow) her mother's advice to think sleepy thoughts.

_____ 19. Then she found herself (wrap) her arms around a big teddy bear.

_____ 20. Suddenly she woke up and knew she'd have an (amuse) story to tell about not sleeping!

Notes for Home: Your child spelled words that have *-ed, -ing, -er,* or *-est* endings. **Home Activity:** Think of base words that are regular verbs *(jump, play)* or adjectives *(soft, tall)*. Have your child add *-ed* or *-ing* to the verbs and *-er* or *-est* to the adjectives to spell new words.

Spelling: Adding -ed and -ing, -er and -est

Directions: Proofread the letter. Find seven spelling mistakes.
Use the proofreading marks to correct each mistake.

≡	Make a capital.
/	Make a small letter.
∧	Add something.
✗	Take out something.
⊙	Add a period.
¶	Begin a new paragraph.

Dear Lucy,

   Yesterday I took my first airplane ride by myself. It was

really exiting. I tryed to act very grown-up. Next to me was a

lady with the cutest baby boy. The baby was all wraped up. I

got to hold him. He felt lightter than a feather! Then he threw

up on me. I pretended to be amuzed, but really it was gross.

Folowing dinner was a movie. We arrived in Chicago half an hour

earlier than expected. Flying is easyer than I thought!

                         Your friend,

                         Karen

Proofread and Write

Spelling Tip
Words that end in -y
If a base word ends in a **consonant** and **y**, change
the **y** to **i** before adding **-ed, -er,** or **-est.** Keep the **y**
when adding **-ing.** For example: **try, tried, trying.**

Write a Letter
On a separate sheet of paper, write a letter Lucy might
write back to Karen telling how she achieved something
all by herself. Try to use at least six of your spelling
words.

Word List
followed	amused
following	amusing
lighter	bigger
lightest	biggest
tried	wrapped
trying	wrapping
cuter	earlier
cutest	earliest
excited	easier
exciting	easiest

Notes for Home: Your child spelled words that end in *-ed, -ing, -er,* or *-est.* **Home Activity:**
Look at video boxes, mail, or magazines to find words with these endings. Help figure out
whether the spelling of the base word was changed before the ending was added.

Spelling: Adding -ed and -ing, -er and -est

REVIEW

Word List				
followed	tried	excited	bigger	earlier
following	trying	exciting	biggest	earliest
lighter	cuter	amused	wrapped	easier
lightest	cutest	amusing	wrapping	easiest

Directions: Choose the word from the box that is most opposite in meaning for each word below. Write the word on the line.

1. uglier _____

2. later _____

3. smaller _____

4. heavier _____

5. smallest _____

6. bored _____

7. led _____

8. harder _____

9. leading _____

10. hardest _____

Directions: Choose the word from the box that best completes each person's statement. Write the word on the line to the left.

_____ 11. Fast Food Worker: "Our food comes hot, _____ in foil, and ready to go."

_____ 12. Comedian: "Most people find me _____."

_____ 13. Child Actor: "Everyone says I have the _____ baby face."

_____ 14. News Photographer: "My work often takes me to _____ places."

_____ 15. Athlete: "I keep _____ to break records in my sport."

_____ 16. Store Clerk: "I'm always _____ presents for people."

_____ 17. School Bus Driver: "I have to be the _____ person awake at my house."

_____ 18. Jockey: "The _____ jockey on the fastest horse usually wins the race."

_____ 19. Politician: "I _____ my best to get elected."

_____ 20. Clown: "Are you _____ by my funny costume?"

Notes for Home: Your child spelled words that end in *-ed, -ing, -er,* or *-est.* **Home Activity:** Ask your child to explain why the base words of some spelling words were changed before an ending was added, such as *cute/cutest, big/bigger,* and *try/tried.*

Spelling: Vowels with No Sound Clues

Pretest Directions: Fold back the page along the dotted line. On the blanks, write the spelling words as they are dictated. When you have finished the test, unfold the page and check your words.

1._____

2._____

3._____

4._____

5._____

6._____

7._____

8._____

9._____

10._____

11._____

12._____

13._____

14._____

15._____

16._____

17._____

18._____

19._____

20._____

1. The store's **manager** helped us.

2. We will elect a class **president**.

3. There is a **different** way.

4. What a **terrible** storm!

5. I **finally** finished the book.

6. This is **really** the place.

7. Are you **supposed** to do that?

8. There will **probably** be more.

9. **California** is a populous state.

10. She **especially** likes pears.

11. Don't lose your **balance**.

12. There was a **constant** noise.

13. She proved herself **innocent**.

14. I did not **realize** it was so far.

15. This is a wonderful **opportunity**.

16. Cars **pollute** the air.

17. The **prisoner** was in jail.

18. We will **celebrate** your birthday.

19. We buy milk at the **grocery** store.

20. The **elevator** does not work.

Notes for Home: Your child took a pretest on words whose vowel sounds have no sound clues. *Home Activity:* Help your child learn misspelled words before the final test. Have your child divide misspelled words into parts (such as syllables) and concentrate on each part.

Think and Practice

Spelling: Vowels with No Sound Clues

Word List				
manager	finally	California	innocent	prisoner
president	really	especially	realize	celebrate
different	supposed	balance	opportunity	grocery
terrible	probably	constant	pollute	elevator

Directions: Choose the three-syllable words from the box. Write the words in in alphabetical order. Draw lines between syllables.

1. _____   7. _____

2. _____   8. _____

3. _____   9. _____

4. _____   10. _____

5. _____   11. _____

6. _____   12. _____

Directions: Choose the word from the box that best matches each clue. Write the word on the line.

_____ 13. You ride one of these to get to the top of a building.

_____ 14. You do this if you throw a piece of trash in the river.

_____ 15. This means almost the same as "chance."

_____ 16. This is something that stays the same without changing.

_____ 17. A gymnast needs to have this if she doesn't want to fall.

_____ 18. This is a large state along the western coast of the United States.

_____ 19. This means almost the same as "expected" or "required."

_____ 20. You might use this word instead of *very* to show that something is special.

Notes for Home: Your child spelled words with unstressed vowel sounds that give no clue to their spelling, such as *grocery*. **Home Activity:** On a sheet of paper, write the consonants of each spelling word and leave blanks for the vowels. Challenge your child to fill in the vowels.

Spelling: Vowels with No Sound Clues

Directions: Proofread the student announcement. Find seven spelling mistakes. Use the proofreading marks to correct each mistake.

Roosevelt High School will celebrat its new

playing field with a special Track and Field

Day on October 24. Students will have the

oportunety to compete in many diferent

events. Prizes will be given and refreshments

served. It should be a reelly fun day. Rain

date: October 25. (But only if the weather is

espeshally terible.) Come and realize your

potential on Track and Field Day!

≡	Make a capital.
/	Make a small letter.
∧	Add something.
℘	Take out something.
⊙	Add a period.
¶	Begin a new paragraph.

Spelling Tip
Spelling schwa
Sometimes knowing a base word can help you remember how to spell the schwa sound, the unstressed vowel sound that gives no clue to its spelling. Example: Something that **diff**e**rs** is **diff**e**rent.**

Word List

manager	really	balance	pollute
president	supposed	constant	prisoner
different	probably	innocent	celebrate
terrible	California	realize	grocery
finally	especially	opportunity	elevator

Write an Announcement

On a separate sheet of paper, write an announcement for a real or imaginary event. Try to use at least five of your spelling words.

Notes for Home: Your child spelled words with unstressed vowel sounds that give no clue to their spelling, such as *grocery*. **Home Activity:** Write each spelling word in a list, misspelling several words. Have your child check and correct the list.

© Scott Foresman 5

Spelling: Vowels with No Sound Clues

REVIEW

Word List				
manager	finally	California	innocent	prisoner
president	really	especially	realize	celebrate
different	supposed	balance	opportunity	grocery
terrible	probably	constant	pollute	elevator

Directions: Choose the word from the box that best completes each statement. Write the word on the line to the left.

_____ 1. *City* is to *Los Angeles* as *state* is to _____.

_____ 2. *Hot* is to *cold* as *guilty* is to _____.

_____ 3. *Castle* is to *king* as *White House* is to _____.

_____ 4. *Automobile* is to *car* as *market* is to _____.

_____ 5. *Big* is to *little* as *same* is to _____.

_____ 6. *Cage* is to *bird* as *jail* is to _____.

_____ 7. *Child* is to *parent* as *worker* is to _____.

_____ 8. *Sad* is to *mourn* as *happy* is to _____.

_____ 9. *Build* is to *destroy* as *clean* is to _____.

_____ 10. *Sure* is to *certain* as *awful* is to _____.

_____ 11. *Unequal* is to *equal* as *imbalance* is to _____.

_____ 12. *Usual* is to *usually* as *final* is to _____.

Directions: Choose the word from the box that best replaces the underlined word or words. Write the word on the line.

_____ 13. You are <u>required</u> to run every day when in training.

_____ 14. If the weather is <u>always the same</u>, you can run outdoors daily.

_____ 15. Dedicated runners take every <u>good chance</u> to run.

_____ 16. Skip riding the <u>mechanical car that lifts</u> and take the stairs.

_____ 17. People don't <u>understand</u> how important proper nutrition is.

_____ 18. Eating right is <u>actually</u> just as important as working out.

_____ 19. It is <u>particularly</u> important to avoid foods that are high in fat.

_____ 20. If you eat right and train hard, you will <u>most likely</u> succeed.

Notes for Home: Your child spelled words with unstressed vowel sounds that give no clue to their spelling, such as *grocery*. **Home Activity:** Write each word on an index card. Draw a card, read it aloud, and have your child spell it. Switch roles and repeat.

Spelling: Vowels in Final Syllables

Pretest Directions: Fold back the page along the dotted line. On the blanks, write the spelling words as they are dictated. When you have finished the test, unfold the page and check your words.

1._____

2._____

3._____

4._____

5._____

6._____

7._____

8._____

9._____

10._____

11._____

12._____

13._____

14._____

15._____

16._____

17._____

18._____

19._____

20._____

1. I do not want **either** one.

2. Read me **another** story.

3. Th school has a new **computer**.

4. Hang the **calendar** on the wall.

5. I drew a map of the **solar** system.

6. Which place in **particular** is it?

7. Good is the opposite of **evil**.

8. We found a **fossil** of a fern.

9. To be polite is to be **civil**.

10. Please **cancel** my subscription.

11. The **label** on the bottle is red.

12. May I change the **channel**?

13. The twins had a bad **quarrel**.

14. Have you **eaten** yet?

15. I do not like **frozen** vegetables.

16. The fire engine has a loud **siren**.

17. She opened the **curtain**.

18. Who is the ship's **captain**?

19. I threw coins in the **fountain**.

20. His father always gets a **bargain**.

Notes for Home: Your child took a pretest on how to spell the vowel sound in final syllables. *Home Activity:* Help your child learn misspelled words before the final test. See if there are any similar errors and discuss a memory trick that could help.

Spelling: Vowels in Final Syllables

Think and Practice

Word List

either	particular	label	siren
another	evil	channel	curtain
computer	fossil	quarrel	captain
calendar	civil	eaten	fountain
solar	cancel	frozen	bargain

Directions: Choose the words from the box that have a final syllable that sounds like the final syllable in **open.** Write each word in the correct column.

Final syllable spelled -ain

1. _____

2. _____

3. _____

4. _____

Final syllable spelled -en

5. _____

6. _____

7. _____

Directions: Each word below has a letter missing. Decide which vowel—**e, i,** or **a**—to add to each word to form a word from the box. Write the word on the line.

8. lab_l _____

9. anoth_r _____

10. sol_r _____

11. civ_l _____

12. quarr_l _____

13. particul_r _____

14. eith_r _____

15. ev_l _____

16. comput_r _____

17. chann_l _____

18. foss_l _____

19. calend_r _____

20. canc_l _____

Notes for Home: Your child spelled words with indistinct vowel sounds in their final syllables that sound alike but are spelled differently, such as *solar* and *either.* **Home Activity:** Give your child clues about each spelling word. Have him or her guess and spell the word.

Spelling: Vowels in Final Syllables

Directions: Proofread the book review. Find seven spelling mistakes. Use the proofreading marks to correct each mistake.

≡	Make a capital.
/	Make a small letter.
∧	Add something.
❨	Take out something.
⊙	Add a period.
¶	Begin a new paragraph.

BETWEEN A BOOK'S COVERS

Memories of My Travels, by Captain Ronald Tweet, is filled with tales of the famous explorer's adventures. In one chapter, he tells of his search for the fossel of a forgotten dinosaur. In another, he describes his quest for the fountin of youth in India, where he had a close call with death after he had eaten a two-month old sandwich! On an expedition to the frozin lands of the North Pole, Sir Ronald's ship almost sinks in a dangerous chanel. My particuler favorite is his foolish quarrell with a huge anaconda in the Amazon. If you like excitement, you'll love this book. It's a bargen at $11.95!

Spelling Tip

another
If you have trouble spelling **another,** remember that it's made up of three words: **a not her.**

Word List
either
another
computer
calendar
solar
particular
evil
fossil
civil
cancel
label
channel
quarrel
eaten
frozen
siren
curtain
captain
fountain
bargain

Write a Review

On a separate sheet of paper, write a review of a book, movie, or television program you have recently read or watched. Try to use at least six of your spelling words.

Notes for Home: Your child spelled words with indistinct vowel sounds in their final syllables that sound alike but are spelled differently. *Home Activity:* With your child, sort the spelling words into separate lists according to how their final syllables are spelled.

Spelling: Vowels in Final Syllables ★ REVIEW

Word List				
either	solar	civil	quarrel	curtain
another	particular	cancel	eaten	captain
computer	evil	label	frozen	fountain
calendar	fossil	channel	siren	bargain

Directions: Choose the word from the box that best matches each clue.
Write the word on the line.

_____ **1.** This refers to rights of citizens, such as the right to vote.

_____ **2.** It tells the date.

_____ **3.** It's the opposite of *good*.

_____ **4.** You do this when you can't meet someone as planned.

_____ **5.** It can be one or the other.

_____ **6.** You might dig for one.

_____ **7.** You might find it at a yard sale.

_____ **8.** It has a keyboard and a monitor attached to it.

_____ **9.** This kind of power comes from the sun.

_____ **10.** It's something you change on the television set.

_____ **11.** It appears on packaged foods.

Directions: Choose the word from the box that best completes each sentence.
Write the word on the line to the left.

_____ **12.** There was one day in _____ that I'll never forget.

_____ **13.** We had just _____ lunch.

_____ **14.** We ate _____ fish sticks that we had thawed and baked.

_____ **15.** Suddenly we heard a loud police _____.

_____ **16.** We all ran to the window and pulled back the _____.

_____ **17.** The police were hauling a soaking wet man out of the _____.

_____ **18.** _____ man had pushed him in the town's fountain.

_____ **19.** They had apparently had a _____.

_____ **20.** A police _____ took both men down to the station.

Notes for Home: Your child spelled words with indistinct vowel sounds in their final
syllables that sound alike but are spelled differently, such as *solar* and *either*. **Home Activity:**
Give your child clues to a spelling word. Have him or her guess the word and spell it.

Spelling: Words with *ng, nk, th*

Pretest Directions: Fold back the page along the dotted line. On the blanks, write the spelling words as they are dictated. When you have finished the test, unfold the page and check your words.

1._____
2._____
3._____
4._____
5._____
6._____
7._____
8._____
9._____
10._____
11._____
12._____
13._____
14._____
15._____
16._____
17._____
18._____
19._____
20._____

1. The weightlifter is **strong**.
2. I brought **nothing** to the party.
3. **Everything** happened at once.
4. This **clothing** is expensive.
5. You are **among** friends.
6. Wasps might **sting** a dog.
7. Put your coat on a **hanger**.
8. The **lightning** was very bright.
9. Fill in the **blank**.
10. Open the **trunk** of the car.
11. We ate a lot on **Thanksgiving**.
12. The **chipmunk** buries a nut.
13. The sweater will **shrink**.
14. **They** talked for a long time.
15. There were no cars **then**.
16. We drove **north**.
17. I lost my watch **there**.
18. Do not come **without** her.
19. I walked **though** I was tired.
20. She **thought** it was hers.

Notes for Home: Your child took a pretest on words that include *ng, nk,* or *th.* **Home Activity:** Help your child learn misspelled words before the final test. Your child should look at the word, say it, spell it aloud, and then spell it with eyes shut.

© Scott Foresman 5

Think and Practice

Spelling: Words with *ng, nk, th*

Word List

strong	among	blank	shrink	there
nothing	sting	trunk	they	without
everything	hanger	Thanksgiving	then	though
clothing	lightning	chipmunk	north	thought

Directions: Choose the one-syllable words from the box. Write each word in the correct column.

Contains ng

1. _____

2. _____

Contains nk

3. _____

4. _____

5. _____

Contains th

6. _____

7. _____

8. _____

9. _____

10. _____

11. _____

Directions: Write the word from the box that is associated with each word or words.

12. thunder _____

13. squirrel _____

14. zero _____

15. fashion _____

16. hook _____

17. lacking _____

18. one of _____

19. turkey _____

20. all _____

Notes for Home: Your child spelled words that have *ng, nk,* or *th.* **Home Activity:** Challenge your child to identify the four spelling words that are compound words and use each in a sentence.

Name _____

Spelling: Words with *ng, nk, th*

Directions: Proofread this description. Find six spelling mistakes. Use the proofreading marks to correct each mistake.

☰	Make a capital.
/	Make a small letter.
∧	Add something.
✍	Take out something.
⊙	Add a period.
¶	Begin a new paragraph.

Next week my Grandmother is taking me to the city to see a parade celebrating Independence Day. Nothin is better than visiting the big city. Evrything their is so exciting and fast paced. I tought that I should wear red, white, and blue for the parade. In an old trunck in the attic of my house, I found the perfect costume. Finally the big day arrived. As the parade began, a bolt of lighting lit up the sky. I was worried that the parade might be canceled, but the storm passed and the parade continued. I truly enjoyed my day in the city.

Word List

strong	among	blank	shrink	there
nothing	sting	trunk	they	without
everything	hanger	Thanksgiving	then	though
clothing	lightning	chipmunk	north	thought

Write a Description

On a separate sheet of paper, write a description of something mysterious or strange. It might be a tree, a house, or an animal. You can write from experience or use your imagination. Try to use at least five of your spelling words.

Spelling Tip
there
People often mix up **there** and **their.** Remember the **here** in **there.** Both **here** and **there** refer to **where.**

Notes for Home: Your child practiced writing spelling words that contain the consonants *ng, nk,* or *th.* **Home Activity:** Help your child think of additional words that begin or end with the letters *th.* Make a list of these words.

Spelling: Words with *ng, nk, th*

Word List				
strong	among	blank	shrink	there
nothing	sting	trunk	they	without
everything	hanger	Thanksgiving	then	though
clothing	lightning	chipmunk	north	thought

Directions: Choose the word from the box that begins and ends with the same letter as each word below. Write the word on the line.

1. entering _____

2. workout _____

3. listening _____

4. napping _____

5. today _____

6. thorough _____

7. aging _____

8. tease _____

Directions: Choose the word from the box that best completes each person's statement. Write the word on the line.

_____ 9. Mother: "Put your coat on this _____."

_____ 10. Department Store Clerk: "Take a look at our new line of _____."

_____ 11. Beekeeper: "Sometimes I'm not careful and I get a bee _____."

_____ 12. Forest Ranger: "I have a pet _____ that I feed daily."

_____ 13. Wrestler: "You have to be _____ in my line of work."

_____ 14. Elephant: "I feed myself with my _____."

_____ 15. Trail Guide: "I don't need a compass to find _____."

_____ 16. Writer: "I just _____ of a great idea for my next book."

_____ 17. Artist: "I love filling up a _____ canvas."

_____ 18. Dry Cleaner: "I have to be careful not to _____ my customers' clothes."

_____ 19. Storyteller: "And _____ they lived happily ever after."

_____ 20. Turkey Farmer: "My favorite holiday is _____."

Notes for Home: Your child spelled words with *ng, nk,* and *th*. **Home Activity:** With your child, take turns making up tongue twisters using words that contain *th*. (Example: *Theo threw the third throw through the window.*)

Spelling: Suffixes -able, -ible, -ant, -ent

Pretest Directions: Fold back the page along the dotted line. On the blanks, write the spelling words as they are dictated. When you have finished the test, unfold the page and check your words.

1._____

2._____

3._____

4._____

5._____

6._____

7._____

8._____

9._____

10._____

11._____

12._____

13._____

14._____

15._____

16._____

17._____

18._____

19._____

20._____

1. This is a **comfortable** chair.

2. That is a **reasonable** question.

3. His shirt is hand **washable**.

4. Are you **agreeable** to the plan?

5. She owns a **valuable** painting.

6. Who is **responsible** for you?

7. I saw a **convertible** car go by.

8. The hose is **flexible**.

9. Jane is a very **sensible** person.

10. He bought a **reversible** jacket.

11. That **contestant** won the game.

12. Are you **defiant** of my orders?

13. A detective must be **observant**.

14. Their **servant** has her own car.

15. The house has a new **occupant**.

16. The **student** won an award.

17. I received an **urgent** letter.

18. We are **confident** we will win.

19. He is a **resident** of San Antonio.

20. My **opponent** played well.

Notes for Home: Your child took a pretest on words that have the suffixes *-able, -ible, -ant,* and *-ent*. **Home Activity:** Help your child learn misspelled words before the final test. Your child can underline the word parts that caused the problems and concentrate on those parts.

Think and Practice

Spelling: Suffixes -able, -ible, -ant, -ent

Word List				
comfortable	valuable	sensible	observant	urgent
reasonable	responsible	reversible	servant	confident
washable	convertible	contestant	occupant	resident
agreeable	flexible	defiant	student	opponent

Directions: Choose the words from the box that have the suffixes **-able** and **-ible.** Write each word in the correct column.

Words with -able

1. _____

2. _____

3. _____

4. _____

5. _____

Words with -ible

6. _____

7. _____

8. _____

9. _____

10. _____

Directions: Choose the word from the box that best matches each clue. Write the word on the line.

_____ 11. someone who enters a contest

_____ 12. a person who occupies a place

_____ 13. someone who serves

_____ 14. a person who studies

_____ 15. watchful, quick to notice

_____ 16. the person who resides in a place

_____ 17. something that needs immediate attention

_____ 18. disobedient

_____ 19. a person or group on the opposite side in a game or debate

_____ 20. very sure of yourself

Notes for Home: Your child spelled words that end with *-able, -ible, -ant,* and *-ent.* **Home Activity:** Start to spell each word slowly, one letter at a time. When your child recognizes the word, have him or her say the whole word and then spell it.

Spelling: Suffixes -able, -ible, -ant, -ent

Directions: Proofread this speech. Find five spelling mistakes.
Use the proofreading marks to correct each mistake.

≡	Make a capital.
/	Make a small letter.
∧	Add something.
ℒ	Take out something.
⊙	Add a period.
¶	Begin a new paragraph.

*Ladies and gentlemen, I am an opponant of slavery
who brings you an urgent message today. No servent can
be comfortable as a forced resident or occupent in a home
that is not agreeable. As responsable and sensible people, we
must admit that slavery is not reasonible nor humane. Free
all slaves, because freedom is valuable to all people!*

Spelling Tip

For base words that end in
e, drop the **e** before adding
the suffixes **-able, -ible,
-ant,** and **-ent.** For most
words that end in **y,** change
the **y** to an **i** and then add
the suffix.

Word List

comfortable	responsible	contestant	student
reasonable	convertible	defiant	urgent
washable	flexible	observant	confident
agreeable	sensible	servant	resident
valuable	reversible	occupant	opponent

Write a Speech

Imagine you were asked to give a speech about a
subject you feel strongly about. On a separate sheet of
paper, write the speech you would deliver. Try to use
at least five of your spelling words.

Notes for Home: Your child spelled words that end with *-able, -ible, -ant,* and *-ent.* **Home
Activity:** Spell each spelling word for your child, but purposely make one or more letters
wrong. See if your child can recognize each error and spell the word correctly.

Spelling: Suffixes -able, -ible, -ant, -ent

REVIEW

Word List				
comfortable	valuable	sensible	observant	urgent
reasonable	responsible	reversible	servant	confident
washable	convertible	contestant	occupant	resident
agreeable	flexible	defiant	student	opponent

Directions: Complete each equation to spell a word from the box. Write each word on the line.

1. serve – e + ant = _____

2. observe – e + ant = _____

3. urge – e + ent = _____

4. study – y + ent = _____

5. defy – y + i + ant = _____

6. confide – e + ent = _____

7. occupy – y + ant = _____

8. reside – e + ent = _____

9. contest + ant = _____

10. flex + ible = _____

Directions: Choose the word from the box that best completes each sentence. Write the word on the line to the left.

_____ 11. Car Salesperson: You can buy this car at a very _____ price.

_____ 12. Home Owner: I'll find out who's _____ for this broken window!

_____ 13. Clothing Store Clerk: You'll love this _____ jacket. It's green on one side and purple on the other.

_____ 14. Grandmother: Do you need another blanket, dear, or are you _____ now?

_____ 15. Team Captain: If it's _____ to everyone, we'll meet for practice at 10:00 A.M.

_____ 16. Detective: Someone has stolen a very _____ diamond necklace!

_____ 17. Scout Leader: If you get lost, the _____ thing to do is to follow the creek.

_____ 18. Baby Sitter: Oh, no! I thought the walls were all _____.

_____ 19. Driver: Let's put down the top on the _____ and drive it.

_____ 20. Chess player: My _____ must make the next move.

Notes for Home: Your child spelled words that end with *-able, -ible, -ant,* and *-ent*. **Home Activity:** Read a newspaper article with your child. Together, see how many words you can find that have the ending *-able, -ible, -ant,* or *-ent.*

Spelling: Suffixes -ous, -ion, -ation

Pretest Directions: Fold back the page along the dotted line. On the blanks, write the spelling words as they are dictated. When you have finished the test, unfold the page and check your words.

1. _____

2. _____

3. _____

4. _____

5. _____

6. _____

7. _____

8. _____

9. _____

10. _____

11. _____

12. _____

13. _____

14. _____

15. _____

16. _____

17. _____

18. _____

19. _____

20. _____

1. He is a **famous** writer.

2. Barking dogs make him **nervous**.

3. They sang a **joyous** song.

4. What a **marvelous** idea!

5. That was a **humorous** joke.

6. A **mysterious** man entered.

7. The boat is not **dangerous**.

8. There is a **selection** of pens.

9. She is taking speech **instruction**.

10. He has an **attraction** to parks.

11. Everyone hates **rejection**.

12. A good **education** is valuable.

13. It costs more due to **inflation**.

14. I made a **decoration**.

15. The police took our **information**.

16. This project needs **organization**.

17. They had a nice **conversation**.

18. You have a vivid **imagination**.

19. He has our **admiration**.

20. The plan takes **preparation**.

Notes for Home: Your child took a pretest on words that have the suffixes *-ous, -ion,* and *-ation.* **Home Activity:** Help your child learn misspelled words before the final test. Have your child divide misspelled words into parts (such as syllables) and concentrate on each part.

Name_____

Think and Practice

Spelling: Suffixes -ous, -ion, -ation

Word List				
famous	humorous	instruction	inflation	conversation
nervous	mysterious	attraction	decoration	imagination
joyous	dangerous	rejection	information	admiration
marvelous	selection	education	organization	preparation

Directions: Add the suffix **-ion** or **-ation** to form a word from the box. Write the word on the line. Remember to drop the silent **e** when necessary.

Add -ion

1. instruct _____

2. select _____

3. reject _____

4. attract _____

5. decorate _____

6. educate _____

7. inflate _____

Add -ation

8. inform _____

9. converse _____

10. imagine _____

11. admire _____

12. prepare _____

13. organize _____

Directions: Add the suffix **-ous** to each base word to form a word from the box. Write the letters of each word in the blanks. The boxed letters spell one of the words you wrote, a word that tells how you might feel if you were flying for the first time. Hint: Three words will change spelling before adding **-ous**.

14. danger

15. mystery

16. marvel

17. nerve

18. fame

19. humor

20. joy

14. __ __ [ ] __ __ __ __ __ __

15. __ __ __ [ ] __ __ __ __ __

16. __ __ __ [ ] __ __ __ __

17. __ __ __ [ ] __ __ __

18. __ __ __ [ ] __ __

19. __ __ [ ] __ __ __

20. __ __ __ [ ]

How might you feel on your first flight?

__ __ __ __ __ __ __ __

Notes for Home: Your child spelled words that end in *-ous*, *-ion*, and *-ation*. **Home Activity:** Read a newspaper article with your child. See how many words he or she can recognize that end in *-ous*, *-ion*, or *-ation*.

Spelling: Suffixes -ous, -ion, -ation

Directions: Proofread this story. Find five spelling mistakes. Use the proofreading marks to correct each mistake.

☰	Make a capital.
/	Make a small letter.
∧	Add something.
ℐ	Take out something.
⊙	Add a period.
¶	Begin a new paragraph.

Joey's first trip to the marvelous city of Chicago was a joyus day. He saw famous skyscrapers like the Sears Tower and the Hancock Tower. Joey felt a great admiration for the architect of Chicago's beautiful Union Station. It seemed mystereous to him that any place could be so big.

While they were in the Art Institute, Joey's mother struck up a conversatioun with one of the guards. He shared some helpful informacion about which elevator would take them to the special exhibit. The paintings there gave Joey more educcation than he ever got in a classroom!

Word List

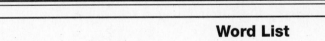

famous	humorous	instruction	inflation	conversation
nervous	mysterious	attraction	decoration	imagination
joyous	dangerous	rejection	information	admiration
marvelous	selection	education	organization	preparation

Write a Story

On a separate sheet of paper, write a paragraph describing things you saw on a trip to the city. Try to use at least five of your spelling words.

Spelling Tip

marvelous

How can you remember that **marvelous** has an **o** before the **u**? Think of this hint: Oh, **you (o-u)** look **marvel<u>ous</u>!**

Notes for Home: Your child spelled words that end in -*ous*, -*ion*, and -*ation*. **Home Activity:** Say each spelling word to your child. Have him or her identify whether it ends in -*ous*, -*ion*, or -*ation*. Then have your child spell the word.

Proofread and Write

Spelling: Suffixes -ous, -ion, -ation   REVIEW

Word List

famous	humorous	instruction	inflation	conversation
nervous	mysterious	attraction	decoration	imagination
joyous	dangerous	rejection	information	admiration
marvelous	selection	education	organization	preparation

Directions: Choose the word from the box that best matches each clue.
Write the word on the line.

_____ **1.** It's a talk between two or more people.

_____ **2.** It's a group of people who work together.

_____ **3.** It's what you use to create interesting make-believe stories.

_____ **4.** It's what you do to get ready.

_____ **5.** It's being turned down or turned away.

_____ **6.** It's what happens when a magnet is near metal.

_____ **7.** It's often seen on top of a cake.

_____ **8.** It's what happens to a balloon that's blown up.

_____ **9.** It's a choice that you make.

_____ **10.** It's what a person feels for a hero or idol.

_____ **11.** It's what you find in any encyclopedia article.

_____ **12.** It's what you get from going to school.

Directions: Choose the word from the box that has the same or nearly the same
meaning as each word below. Write the word on the line.

13. directions _____ **17.** well-known _____

14. strange _____ **18.** happy _____

15. funny _____ **19.** worried _____

16. unsafe _____ **20.** wonderful _____

Notes for Home: Your child spelled words that end in *-ous*, *-ion*, and *-ation*. **Home Activity:**
Say each spelling word without the suffix. Have your child add the proper suffix and spell the
word.

© Scott Foresman 5

Spelling: Compound Words 2

Pretest Directions: Fold back the page along the dotted line. On the blanks, write the spelling words as they are dictated. When you have finished the test, unfold the page and check your words.

1. _____
2. _____
3. _____
4. _____
5. _____
6. _____
7. _____
8. _____
9. _____
10. _____
11. _____
12. _____
13. _____
14. _____
15. _____
16. _____
17. _____
18. _____
19. _____
20. _____

1. My **bookshelf** is full.
2. **Someone** ate the apples.
3. **Everybody** came to the party.
4. She is **nowhere** to be found.
5. She wants a chocolate **cupcake**.
6. Eleanor has a new **wristwatch**.
7. **Everyone** is here.
8. We **blindfold** the player.
9. My dad found a **typewriter**.
10. She is my only **grandparent**.
11. The girl hit a **home run**.
12. We are talking to **each other**.
13. I want ketchup on my **hot dog**.
14. Is a window seat **all right**?
15. My sister goes to **high school**.
16. Her **pen pal** lives in Tobago.
17. The stereo is in the **living room**.
18. **Peanut butter** is sticky.
19. **No one** was home when I called.
20. I got **first aid** for my injury.

Notes for Home: Your child took a pretest on compound words. *Home Activity:* Help your child learn misspelled words before the final test. Dictate the word and have your child spell the word aloud for you or write it on paper.

Spelling: Compound Words 2

Think and Practice

Word List				
bookshelf	cupcake	typewriter	hot dog	living room
someone	wristwatch	grandparent	all right	peanut butter
everybody	everyone	home run	high school	no one
nowhere	blindfold	each other	pen pal	first aid

Directions: Choose the compound words from the box that are written as one word. Write the words in alphabetical order on the lines.

1. _____   6. _____

2. _____   7. _____

3. _____   8. _____

4. _____   9. _____

5. _____   10. _____

Directions: Choose the compound word from the box that best completes each sentence. Write the word on the line to the left. Hint: Each compound word is spelled as two words, and one word of the compound word is the same as the underlined word in the sentence.

_____ **11.** The <u>school</u> that I will attend next is _____.

_____ **12.** It is too <u>hot</u> to eat a _____.

_____ **13.** <u>Run</u> around all the bases after hitting a _____.

_____ **14.** I bought a new <u>pen</u> to write to my _____.

_____ **15.** Let's <u>first</u> pack a _____ kit for the camping trip.

_____ **16.** <u>Each</u> day we find ways to help _____.

_____ **17.** I need <u>one</u> helper, but _____ is here right now.

_____ **18.** One food made from the <u>peanut</u> is _____.

_____ **19.** The <u>room</u> where we watch television is the _____.

_____ **20.** I have confidence that <u>all</u> of us will be _____.

Notes for Home: Your child spelled compound words. *Home Activity:* Say one of the words in each compound: for example, say *type* for *typewriter*. Have your child tell you the entire word and spell it.

Spelling: Compound Words 2

Directions: Proofread this paragraph. Find five spelling mistakes.
Use the proofreading marks to correct each mistake.

≡	Make a capital.
/	Make a small letter.
∧	Add something.
℘	Take out something.
⊙	Add a period.
¶	Begin a new paragraph.

Every grand parent of mine helped out in
World War II in some way. Grandpa Joe was
a doctor who gave first aid to every body in
the hospital. Grandpa Gus was a soldier that
noone could beat! Grandma Jane worked in
a war office with her new typewriter.
Grandma Gail became a nurse right after
high-school and made sure wounded
soldiers were allright.

Spelling Tip

How can you remember that **all right** is not spelled **allright?** Remember: There is a space to the **right** of **all** in **all right.**

Word List

bookshelf	cupcake	typewriter	hot dog	living room
someone	wristwatch	grandparent	all right	peanut butter
everybody	everyone	home run	high school	no one
nowhere	blindfold	each other	pen pal	first aid

Write a Paragraph

Imagine that you or someone you know served in World War II. On a separate
sheet of paper, write a paragraph describing what you or the other person did in
the war. Try to use at least five of your spelling words.

Notes for Home: Your child spelled compound words. *Home Activity:* Write each spelling
word with the letters scrambled. See if your child can unscramble each word and spell it
correctly.

Spelling: Compound Words 2

REVIEW

Word List				
bookshelf	cupcake	typewriter	hot dog	living room
someone	wristwatch	grandparent	all right	peanut butter
everybody	everyone	home run	high school	no one
nowhere	blindfold	each other	pen pal	first aid

Directions: Choose the word from the box that best completes each statement. Write the word on the line to the left.

_____ 1. *Football* is to *touchdown* as *baseball* is to _____.

_____ 2. *Ears* are to *earplugs* as *eyes* are to _____.

_____ 3. *School* is to *gymnasium* as *house* is to _____.

_____ 4. *Temperature* is to *thermometer* as *time* is to _____.

_____ 5. *Picnic* is to *sandwich* as *ballgame* is to _____.

_____ 6. *Artist* is to *paintbrush* as *author* is to _____.

_____ 7. *Food* is to *cupboard* as *book* is to _____.

_____ 8. *Salt* is to *pepper* as *jelly* is to _____.

_____ 9. *Mother* is to *parent* as *grandmother* is to _____.

_____ 10. *Doctor* is to *hospital* as *teacher* is to _____.

_____ 11. *Play* is to *teammate* as *write* is to _____.

_____ 12. *Main course* is to *stew* as *dessert* is to _____.

Directions: Unscramble the letters to find a word from the box. Write the word on the line. (Be careful with compounds that are written as two words.)

13. on neo _____

14. bevedyory _____

15. nevereoy _____

16. stirf dai _____

17. ache herot _____

18. lal thrig _____

19. emoneos _____

20. onhewer _____

Notes for Home: Your child spelled compound words. *Home Activity:* See how many more compound words your child can list that contain words found in each spelling word. For example, from *bookshelf* you could get *bookstore, bookmark, bookbag*.

Spelling: Related Words

Pretest Directions: Fold back the page along the dotted line. On the blanks, write the spelling words as they are dictated. When you have finished the test, unfold the page and check your words.

1. _____

2. _____

3. _____

4. _____

5. _____

6. _____

7. _____

8. _____

9. _____

10. _____

11. _____

12. _____

13. _____

14. _____

15. _____

16. _____

17. _____

18. _____

19. _____

20. _____

1. **Please** pass the stuffing.

2. We had a very **pleasant** day.

3. My scarf is made of soft **cloth**.

4. Dirty **clothes** go in the hamper.

5. The **sign** pointed north.

6. She has a lovely **signature**.

7. I had a strange **dream** last night.

8. She **dreamt** she was dancing.

9. My bicycle needs a new **part**.

10. This is only a **partial** list.

11. The cake was rich and **moist**.

12. We **moisten** the stamps.

13. Smoke makes it hard to **breathe**.

14. Take a deep **breath**.

15. His stories **create** new worlds.

16. A toad is an odd **creature**.

17. We will **elect** a new governor.

18. The **election** is tomorrow.

19. You must **practice** every day.

20. Paper shoes are not **practical**.

Notes for Home: Your child took a pretest on pairs of words that have parts spelled the same but pronounced differently. *Home Activity:* Help your child learn misspelled words before the final test by underlining the parts that are different in each pair and concentrating on those.

Spelling: Related Words

Word List				
please	sign	part	breathe	elect
pleasant	signature	partial	breath	election
cloth	dream	moist	create	practice
clothes	dreamt	moisten	creature	practical

Directions: Choose the words from the box that have one syllable. Write each word on a line.

1. _____   6. _____

2. _____   7. _____

3. _____   8. _____

4. _____   9. _____

5. _____   10. _____

Directions: Complete each equation to form a word from the box. Write the word on the line.

11. practice – e + al = _____

12. assign – as + ature = _____

13. moisture – ure + en = _____

14. depart – de + ial = _____

15. please – e + ant = _____

16. select – s + ion = _____

17. create – e + ure = _____

18. practical – al + e = _____

19. creation – ion + e = _____

20. election – ion = _____

Notes for Home: Your child spelled pairs of words that have parts that are spelled the same but pronounced differently. ***Home Activity:*** Say a spelling word aloud. Have your child say the related word and spell it for you. Repeat for other pairs of related words.

Name _____

Spelling: Related Words

Directions: Proofread this diary entry. Find five spelling mistakes. Use the proofreading marks to correct each mistake.

≡	Make a capital.
/	Make a small letter.
∧	Add something.
✓	Take out something.
⊙	Add a period.
¶	Begin a new paragraph.

July 4, 1776.

Dear Diary: Today every leader in Congress will put his sigature on a document that will create a new nation—the United States! I used to think independence was only a dream, but now it's practicle and real! Now we can elect our own leaders, which will pleaze all Americans. It's like a breathe of fresh air! Today I'll wear my best cloths!

Spelling Tip

breath   **breathe**

How can you remember the difference between **breath** and **breathe?** Think of this hint: You **breathe the** air.

Word List

please	moist
pleasant	moisten
cloth	breathe
clothes	breath
sign	create
signature	creature
dream	elect
dreamt	election
part	practice
partial	practical

Write a Diary Entry

Imagine you were an American colonist at the time of the Revolutionary War. Write a diary entry that describes your experiences or your feelings about the war. Try to use at least five of your spelling words.

Notes for Home: Your child spelled pairs of words that have parts that are spelled the same but pronounced differently. *Home Activity:* Write one word for each pair of related spelling words. Have your child show how the word can be changed to spell a related word.

Name _____

Spelling: Related Words

REVIEW

Word List				
please	sign	part	breathe	elect
pleasant	signature	partial	breath	election
cloth	dream	moist	create	practice
clothes	dreamt	moisten	creature	practical

Directions: Choose the word from the box that best completes each sentence. Write the word on the line to the right.

In 1775, American colonists felt that life under English rule was harsh, not **1.** _____. Colonists could not **2.** _____ their own leaders. War seemed to be the only **3.** _____ way to win their freedom. But with untrained soldiers, victory seemed like a distant **4.** _____. After some **5.** _____, however, the soldiers got better. Soon the colonists were able to **6.** _____ a sigh of relief. In 1776, American leaders agreed to **7.** _____ a Declaration of Independence. They would **8.** _____ a new nation—the United States of America. Later, they held an **9.** _____ and George Washington became president in 1789.

1. _____
2. _____
3. _____
4. _____
5. _____
6. _____
7. _____
8. _____
9. _____

Directions: Choose the word from the box that belongs in each group of words. Write the word on the line.

10. gasp, sigh, _____

11. fantasized, imagined, _____

12. piece, portion, _____

13. thank you, excuse me, _____

14. animal, beast, _____

15. dampen, rinse, _____

16. autograph, written name, _____

17. humid, damp, _____

18. incomplete, unfinished, _____

19. shoes, hats, _____

20. leather, plastic, _____

Notes for Home: Your child spelled pairs of words that have parts that are spelled the same but pronounced differently. **Home Activity:** Together, see if you and your child can name more words that are related to each pair. For example, *create* and *creature* are also related to *creation*.

Spelling: Easily Confused Words

Pretest Directions: Fold back the page along the dotted line. On the blanks, write the spelling words as they are dictated. When you have finished the test, unfold the page and check your words.

1._____
2._____
3._____
4._____
5._____
6._____
7._____
8._____
9._____
10._____
11._____
12._____
13._____
14._____
15._____
16._____
17._____
18._____
19._____
20._____

1. This is the last **of** the oranges.
2. Please turn **off** the lamp.
3. I like all fruit **except** bananas.
4. I didn't **accept** the invitation.
5. **Which** is the way to town?
6. She was a **witch** for Halloween.
7. **Where** is the grocery store?
8. We **were** lost in the hills.
9. The **weather** was stormy.
10. Tell me **whether** you will come.
11. He has a **plant** with red flowers.
12. They saw a new **planet**.
13. The ball went out of **bounds**.
14. The girls **bounce** the ball.
15. Camels live in the **desert**.
16. We will have cake for **dessert**.
17. The sun will **rise** soon.
18. They **raise** the flags up high.
19. What is for **dinner**?
20. This **diner** serves malts.

Notes for Home: Your child took a pretest on words easily confused with another word.
Home Activity: Help your child learn misspelled words. Your child should look at the word in its sentence, think about its meaning, spell it aloud, and then spell it with eyes shut.

Name_____

Spelling: Easily Confused Words

Think and Practice

Word List				
of	which	weather	bounds	rise
off	witch	whether	bounce	raise
except	where	plant	desert	dinner
accept	were	planet	dessert	diner

Directions: Choose the word from the box that is easily confused with the word given. Write the word on the line.

1. off _____

2. except _____

3. which _____

4. where _____

5. weather _____

6. plant _____

7. bounds _____

8. dessert _____

9. rise _____

10. dinner _____

Directions: Write the word from the box that belongs in each group of words.

11. leaps, jumps, _____

12. flower, bush, _____

13. under, over, on, _____

14. breakfast, lunch, _____

15. here, there, _____

16. what, who, _____

17. swell, lift, _____

18. exclude, omit, _____

19. snow, rain, _____

20. pie, cake, _____

Notes for Home: Your child spelled words that are easily confused, such as *off* and *of*. **Home Activity:** Help your child think of other pairs of easily confused words, such as *conscience/conscious, adapt/adopt,* and *wreck/wreak.* Invite him or her to spell both words.

Spelling: Easily Confused Words

Directions: Proofread this letter of apology. Find five spelling mistakes. Use the proofreading marks to correct each mistake.

☰	Make a capital.
╱	Make a small letter.
∧	Add something.
⸜	Take out something.
⊙	Add a period.
¶	Begin a new paragraph.

Dear Rita,

   I'm sorry that I yelled at you yesterday. You were right, and I was out of bounds. Please ecept my apology, which is sincere. We could plant some flowers if the whether is nice or go out to diner. I will buy you a nice desert, anything acept strawberry shortcake because I know you don't like it.

                    Your friend,

                    Carlos

Spelling Tip

Remember the number of **s**'s in **dessert** and **desert** this way: **Desserts** are **so sweet**, but a **desert** is only **sandy**.

Write a Letter

On a separate sheet of paper, write a note to a friend in which you settle a conflict or other problem between you. Try to use at least five of your spelling words.

Word List

of	plant
off	planet
except	bounds
accept	bounce
which	desert
witch	dessert
where	rise
were	raise
weather	dinner
whether	diner

Notes for Home: Your child spelled words that are easily confused, such as *off* and *of*. **Home Activity:** Spell each word aloud, pausing between each letter. As soon as your child recognizes the word, have him or her say the word and tell its meaning.

Spelling: Easily Confused Words

REVIEW

Word List

of	which	weather	bounds	rise
off	witch	whether	bounce	raise
except	where	plant	desert	dinner
accept	were	planet	dessert	diner

Directions: Choose the word from the box that best matches each clue. Write the letters of the word on the blanks. The boxed letters answer the riddle: What do you do to place *it* and *run* in alphabetical order?

1. a very dry place

2. a foul ball is out of

3. rubber balls do this

4. atmospheric conditions

5. pledge _____ allegiance

6. Mars, for example

7. sweet item served at the end of a meal

8. a place to eat

9. an important meal

10. an ivy, for example

1. __ __ __ ☐ __ __

2. __ __ ☐ __ __ __

3. __ __ ☐ __ __ __

4. __ ☐ __ __ __ __ __

5. ☐ __

6. __ __ __ __ ☐ __

7. __ __ __ ☐ __ __ __ __

8. __ __ __ ☐ __

9. __ ☐ __ __ __ __

10. __ __ __ __ ☐

What would you do to place it in alphabetical order?

__ __ __   __ __ __ __ __   __ __

Directions: Unscramble the letters to find a word from the box. Write the word on the line.

11. fof _____

12. rheew _____

13. rewe _____

14. itwch _____

15. xetecp _____

16. seira _____

17. wreheth _____

18. pctace _____

19. chiwh _____

20. ires _____

Notes for Home: Your child spelled words that are easily confused, such as *off* and *of*. **Home Activity:** Challenge your child to write a sentence that uses each pair of words together in a single sentence.

Spelling: Using Just Enough Letters

Pretest Directions: Fold back the page along the dotted line. On the blanks, write the spelling words as they are dictated. When you have finished the test, unfold the page and check your words.

1._____	1. Wait **until** tomorrow.
2._____	2. We **went** to the skating rink.
3._____	3. Is that **enough** food for you?
4._____	4. Do you watch too much **TV**?
5._____	5. I have **one** quarter left.
6._____	6. The cat **didn't** like water.
7._____	7. That is **a lot** of ice cream.
8._____	8. The boys **want** to play ball.
9._____	9. The librarian **doesn't** like noise.
10._____	10. The sun **always** sets at night.
11._____	11. Her **necklace** has a diamond.
12._____	12. What is the **exact** time?
13._____	13. The **burglar** wore a mask.
14._____	14. We need the right **equipment**.
15._____	15. The **chimney** is very dirty.
16._____	16. I thought it did not **exist**.
17._____	17. There was a **rumbling** below us.
18._____	18. I painted a cat **upon** the canvas.
19._____	19. She is a great **athlete**.
20._____	20. The doctor will **examine** your cut.

Notes for Home: Your child took a pretest on words that have difficult letter combinations. *Home Activity:* Help your child learn misspelled words before the final test. Your child can underline the word parts that caused the problems and concentrate on those parts.

Spelling: Using Just Enough Letters

Word List

until	one	doesn't	burglar	rumbling
went	didn't	always	equipment	upon
enough	a lot	necklace	chimney	athlete
TV	want	exact	exist	examine

Directions: Choose the words from the box that begin with a vowel. Sort them according to which vowel they start with. Write the words in the correct column.

Begins with a

1. _____

2. _____

3. _____

Begins with u

4. _____

5. _____

Begins with e

6. _____

7. _____

8. _____

9. _____

10. _____

Begins with o

11. _____

Directions: Choose the word from the box that best replaces the underlined word or words. Write the word on the line.

_____ 12. Lauren <u>did not</u> have anything to do.

_____ 13. She decided to watch a science show on <u>television</u>.

_____ 14. When show was over, Lauren <u>left</u> from the room.

_____ 15. "I <u>would like</u> to try an experiment!" she said.

_____ 16. "It <u>does not</u> look hard," she thought.

_____ 17. Lauren put chemicals on an old <u>piece of jewelry worn around the neck</u>.

_____ 18. Smoke from the chemicals drifted up the <u>smokestack over the fireplace</u>.

_____ 19. The experiment started <u>make a deep, rolling sound</u> like thunder.

_____ 20. "Well, I guess a <u>robber</u> won't steal *this* experiment!" she laughed.

Notes for Home: Your child spelled words using just enough letters to spell them correctly.
Home Activity: With your child, practice spelling the words by first pronouncing each word carefully and correctly, syllable by syllable.

Spelling: Using Just Enough Letters

Directions: Proofread this recipe. Find six spelling mistakes. Use the proofreading marks to correct each mistake.

≡	Make a capital.
/	Make a small letter.
∧	Add something.
℘	Take out something.
⊙	Add a period.
¶	Begin a new paragraph.

Salad Surprise

Eqipment: Cutting board, sharp knife, salad bowl

Ingredients: Enuff fresh lettuce to fill bowl; at least three "surprise" ingredients such as mini-crackers, raisins, nuts, or marshmallows; one-half cup bottled dressing.

- Always wash lettuce thoroughly. Examne it closely for bugs.

- Rip lettuce into alot of small pieces. Place in bowl.

- Add other ingredients, on at a time.

- Add dressing and toss untill salad is evenly coated.

Spelling Tip

When you shorten **did not** and **does not** to **didn't** and **doesn't,** you must use apostrophes.

Write a Recipe

On a separate sheet of paper, write a recipe for a dish you have created—or one that you have always dreamed of making! Give it a surprise ingredient or two. Try to use at least five of your spelling words.

Word List

until	necklace
went	exact
enough	burglar
TV	equipment
one	chimney
didn't	exist
a lot	rumbling
want	upon
doesn't	athlete
always	examine

Notes for Home: Your child spelled words using just enough letters to spell them correctly. *Home Activity:* Spell each word for your child, but misspell several words. See if he or she can catch each mistake and spell the word correctly.

Name _____

Spelling: Using Just Enough Letters ⭐ REVIEW

Word List

until	one	doesn't	burglar	rumbling
went	didn't	always	equipment	upon
enough	a lot	necklace	chimney	athlete
TV	want	exact	exist	examine

Directions: Choose the word from the box that best completes each statement. Write the word on the line to the left.

_____ 1. *Knight* is to *armor* as *scuba diver* is to *diving* _____.

_____ 2. *Few* is to *many* as *a little* is to _____.

_____ 3. *Inspector* is to *inspect* as *examiner* is to _____.

_____ 4. *Satisfactory* is to *acceptable* as *sufficient* is to _____.

_____ 5. *Vague* is to *precise* as *inexact* is to _____.

_____ 6. *Knowing* is to *know* as *wanting* is to _____.

_____ 7. *No* is to *yes* as *never* is to _____.

_____ 8. *Is not* is to *isn't* as *does not* is to _____.

_____ 9. *Below* is to *under* as *on* is to _____.

_____ 10. *Wrist* is to *bracelet* as *neck* is to _____.

Directions: Write the word from the box that belongs in each group.

11. sportscaster, coach, _____

12. roaring, crackling, _____

13. radio, video, _____

14. be, live, _____

15. wouldn't, hadn't, _____

16. three, two, _____

17. now, after, _____

18. thief, robber, _____

19. came, saw, _____

20. door, roof, _____

Notes for Home: Your child spelled words using just enough letters to spell them correctly. *Home Activity:* Write each word on a card and show it to your child briefly. Encourage her or him to say each word clearly and picture how the word looks before spelling the word aloud.

Spelling: More Vowels with *r*

Pretest Directions: Fold back the page along the dotted line. On the blanks, write the spelling words as they are dictated. When you have finished the test, unfold the page and check your words.

1._____	1. They became **aware** of a sound.
2._____	2. We have to **prepare** for our trip.
3._____	3. It is nice of you to **share**.
4._____	4. **Declare** your allegiance!
5._____	5. The **spare** tire is flat.
6._____	6. **Beware** of the dog.
7._____	7. Cheese is a **dairy** food.
8._____	8. The **stairway** was dimly lit.
9._____	9. Many bison lived on the **prairie**.
10._____	10. The mechanics **repair** the car.
11._____	11. This book is very **dear** to me.
12._____	12. Their father grew a **beard**.
13._____	13. Lights **appear** in the distance.
14._____	14. The workers were **weary**.
15._____	15. I **smear** the paint on the paper.
16._____	16. The **volunteer** firefighters came.
17._____	17. To be a doctor is a good **career**.
18._____	18. The room looked **cheery**.
19._____	19. He was a true **pioneer**.
20._____	20. **Reindeer** live in Scandinavia.

Notes for Home: Your child took a pretest on words that have vowel sounds with the letter *r*. *Home Activity:* Help your child learn misspelled words before the final test. Dictate the word and have your child spell the word aloud for you or write it on paper.

Spelling: More Vowels with *r*

Word List				
aware	spare	prairie	appear	career
prepare	beware	repair	weary	cheery
share	dairy	dear	smear	pioneer
declare	stairway	beard	volunteer	reindeer

Directions: Choose the words from the box that have the vowel sound with **r** that you hear in **steer**. Sort them according to how the vowel sound is spelled. Write each word in the correct column.

Vowel-r spelled ear

1. _____

2. _____

3. _____

4. _____

5. _____

Vowel-r spelled eer

6. _____

7. _____

8. _____

9. _____

10. _____

Directions: Choose the word from the box that best matches each clue. Write the word on the line.

_____ 11. When you get ready, you do this.

_____ 12. When you fix something, you do this.

_____ 13. A person who knows something is this.

_____ 14. This is a type of farm that produces milk and cheese.

_____ 15. When you give someone part of what you have, you do this.

_____ 16. It's what you call the steps to go upstairs and downstairs.

_____ 17. When you're sure of yourself, you say things this way.

_____ 18. This word signals a warning.

_____ 19. It's something extra, such as a tire in a car.

_____ 20. It's the place where the land is flat.

Notes for Home: Your child spelled words where the letter *r* changes a word's vowel sound, as in *aware* and *cheery*. **Home Activity:** As you read with your child, look for words that have the vowel sound with *r* you hear in *spare* and *dear*.

Name _____

Spelling: More Vowels with *r*

Directions: Proofread this radio announcement. Find seven spelling mistakes. Use the proofreading marks to correct each mistake.

≡	Make a capital.
/	Make a small letter.
∧	Add something.
⌿	Take out something.
⊙	Add a period.
¶	Begin a new paragraph.

Beware! A man with a beerd is playing tricks on people. He can appear anywhere. His usual approach is to offer to repare something, such as a broken starway or window. Then he will smeer paint on it and disappear. He makes a carere out of destructive practical jokes, so stay awear. He is friendly and cheary, but don't be fooled!

Spelling Tip

Watch out for words that have the same vowel sound but different spellings, such as **aware** and **repair,** or **smear** and **career.**

Word List

aware	dear
prepare	beard
share	appear
declare	weary
spare	smear
beware	volunteer
dairy	career
stairway	cheery
prairie	pioneer
repair	reindeer

Write Interview Questions

Imagine you are a reporter. On a separate sheet of paper, write some questions you could ask the man who plays tricks on people. Try to use at least five of your spelling words.

Notes for Home: Your child spelled words where the letter *r* changes a word's vowel sound, as in *aware* and *cheery*. **Home Activity:** Write the spelling words, but leave blanks for the vowel-*r* combinations (*are, air, ear, eer*). Invite your child to fill in the blanks.

Spelling: More Vowels with *r*

Word List

aware	spare	prairie	appear	career
prepare	beware	repair	weary	cheery
share	dairy	dear	smear	pioneer
declare	stairway	beard	volunteer	reindeer

Directions: Choose the word from the box that best replaces the underlined word. Write the word on the line.

_____ 1. My grandmother was an early <u>settler</u> in this region.

_____ 2. Her journey across the <u>plains</u> was long and difficult.

_____ 3. At the end of each day's travel she was <u>tired</u>.

_____ 4. She never did <u>seem</u> to be discouraged, however.

_____ 5. She was always <u>happy</u> and ready to push on.

_____ 6. Once a wheel broke and she was unable to <u>fix</u> it.

_____ 7. Luckily another family had an <u>extra</u> to give her.

_____ 8. In those times, families would always <u>give</u> whatever they had.

_____ 9. They were <u>conscious</u> of the dangers of their journey.

_____ 10. They tried to <u>be ready</u> themselves for anything.

Directions: Choose the word from the box that best matches each clue. Write the word on the line.

_____ 11. These animals pull a holiday sled.

_____ 12. These food products include milk and cheese.

_____ 13. It's what grows on a man's face.

_____ 14. It's what a person does for a living.

_____ 15. It's what you do when you offer your time and help.

_____ 16. It's what a warning sign may say.

_____ 17. It's what babies often do with their food.

_____ 18. It's how you start a friendly letter.

_____ 19. It's what you climb to get to a second floor.

_____ 20. It means almost the same as *say*.

Notes for Home: Your child spelled words where the letter *r* changes a word's vowel sound, as in *aware* and *cheery*. **Home Activity:** Together, write short rhymes using the spelling words. Include other words with the same vowel sounds and spellings.

Spelling: Getting Letters in Correct Order

Pretest Directions: Fold back the page along the dotted line. On the blanks, write the spelling words as they are dictated. When you have finished the test, unfold the page and check your words.

1._____
2._____
3._____
4._____
5._____
6._____
7._____
8._____
9._____
10._____
11._____
12._____
13._____
14._____
15._____
16._____
17._____
18._____
19._____
20._____

1. He is **lonely** without his friends.
2. She owns one **hundred** books.
3. He is my best **friend**.
4. The settlers **built** a cabin.
5. This is a **beautiful** vase.
6. Have you **heard** the news?
7. I heard the news on the **radio**.
8. **Their** feet were getting cold.
9. Who **caught** the most fish?
10. I am **bored** with this program.
11. The **guard** fell asleep.
12. Many people **pierce** their ears.
13. Someone **shrieked** outside.
14. Who will **receive** first prize?
15. What a **horrible** noise!
16. They make **jewelry** for a living.
17. Rocks **tumble** down the hill.
18. We walked to the **northern** cliff.
19. The filed is only half an **acre**.
20. The **museum** is open late.

Notes for Home: Your child took a pretest on words with difficult letter combinations.
Home Activity: Help your child learn misspelled words before the final test. Have your child underline the word parts that caused the problem and concentrate on those parts.

Spelling: Getting Letters in Correct Order

Think and Practice

Word List				
lonely	beautiful	caught	shrieked	tumble
hundred	heard	bored	receive	northern
friend	radio	guard	horrible	acre
built	their	pierce	jewelry	museum

Directions: Choose the words from the box that contain two or more vowels in a row. Sort them according to their vowel pattern. Write each word in the correct column.

Spelled ea or eau

1. _____

2. _____

Spelled ua

3. _____

Spelled io

4. _____

Spelled ei

5. _____

6. _____

Spelled eu

7. _____

Spelled au

8. _____

Spelled ui

9. _____

Spelled ie

10. _____

11. _____

12. _____

Directions: Choose the word from the box that best completes each sentence. Write the word on the line to the left.

_____ 13. My aunt lives on an _____ of land in Maine.

_____ 14. In that _____ state, the winters are long and cold.

_____ 15. My aunt makes beautiful _____ out of sea glass and sells it to tourists in the summer.

_____ 16. She picks which pieces to use by letting the glass gently _____ out of her basket.

_____ 17. She charges as much as one _____ dollars for some pieces.

_____ 18. Some people think that because my aunt works by herself she might be _____.

_____ 19. She loves her work, though, and never gets _____ even when she does the same thing over and over.

_____ 20. Personally, I think it would be _____ to be so isolated, but she likes it.

Notes for Home: Your child spelled words with letter combinations that are often mixed up. *Home Activity:* Write down the spelling words with the letters scrambled. Challenge your child to unscramble the letters to spell each word correctly.

© Scott Foresman 5

Name _____

Spelling: Getting Letters in Correct Order

Directions: Read this e-mail message. Find six spelling mistakes. Use the proofreading marks to correct each mistake.

≡	Make a capital.
/	Make a small letter.
∧	Add something.
ℐ	Take out something.
⊙	Add a period.
¶	Begin a new paragraph.

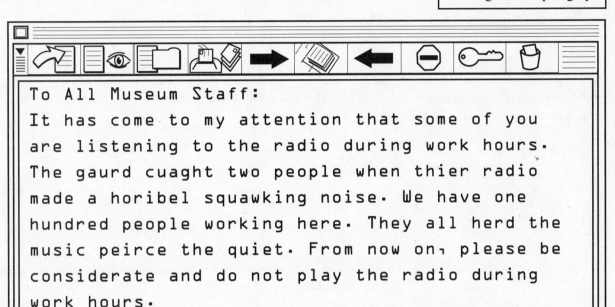

```
To All Museum Staff:
It has come to my attention that some of you
are listening to the radio during work hours.
The gaurd cuaght two people when thier radio
made a horibel squawking noise. We have one
hundred people working here. They all herd the
music peirce the quiet. From now on, please be
considerate and do not play the radio during
work hours.

                              The Management
```

Spelling Tip

jewelry

Many people misspell **jewelry** by mixing up its letters. Remember: there is a **jewel** in **jewel**ry.

Write an E-Mail Message

On a separate sheet of paper, write an e-mail message in which you criticize someone's bad behavior and suggest an alternative. Be constructive, not insulting. Try to use at least four spelling words.

Word List

lonely	guard
hundred	pierce
friend	shrieked
built	receive
beautiful	horrible
heard	jewelry
radio	tumble
their	northern
caught	acre
bored	museum

Notes for Home: Your child spelled words with letter combinations that are often mixed up. *Home Activity:* Have a spelling bee with your child. Take turns saying words from the list for the other person to spell and use in a sentence.

Spelling: Getting Letters in Correct Order

REVIEW

Word List				
lonely	beautiful	caught	shrieked	tumble
hundred	heard	bored	receive	northern
friend	radio	guard	horrible	acre
built	their	pierce	jewelry	museum

Directions: Choose the word from the box that best completes each tongue twister. Write the word on the line to the left. Hint: The answer will start with the same letter as the first word in each sentence.

_____ **1.** Rita would rather _____ a rose from Ralph than Ronald.

_____ **2.** Patty plans to _____ the paper with a pointed pen.

_____ **3.** Fred, a family _____, fried fish for folks at the fair.

_____ **4.** Greg greeted the gabby _____ at the gate.

_____ **5.** Theda and Thelma took _____ three tan tank tops to Tahiti.

_____ **6.** Marcia and Mark managed a _____ of miniature models.

_____ **7.** An _____ offers a lot after all.

_____ **8.** Return the _____ to Rachel for repair.

_____ **9.** Happy Hal has half a _____ hobbies.

_____ **10.** Ten tip-top clowns _____ to tunes together.

Directions: Choose the word from the box that is associated with each word below. Write the word on the line.

11. shriek _____

12. beauty _____

13. bore _____

14. catch _____

15. hear _____

16. horror _____

17. build _____

18. north _____

19. jewel _____

20. lone _____

Notes for Home: Your child spelled words with letter combinations that are often mixed up. *Home Activity:* Help your child create a set of flash cards with these words. Use the cards to help your child practice spelling the words.

© Scott Foresman 5

Spelling: Related Words

Pretest Directions: Fold back the page along the dotted line. On the blanks, write the spelling words as they are dictated. When you have finished the test, unfold the page and check your words.

1._____

2._____

3._____

4._____

5._____

6._____

7._____

8._____

9._____

10._____

11._____

12._____

13._____

14._____

15._____

16._____

17._____

18._____

19._____

20._____

1. He writes a newspaper **column**.

2. My brother is a **columnist**.

3. My **face** is sunburned.

4. Watch her **facial** expressions.

5. My sister has a beautiful **voice**.

6. Her **vocal** cords are sore.

7. The tree **limb** fell in the storm.

8. Athletes keep themselves **limber**.

9. He walks too **fast**.

10. Please **fasten** your seat belt.

11. Grandmother is very **wise**.

12. **Wisdom** comes with experience.

13. The machine finished its **cycle**.

14. My **bicycle** needs a new pedal.

15. We are all **human** beings.

16. Your behavior is quite **humane**.

17. The bridge is not **stable**.

18. **Stability** is difficult to achieve.

19. This is your **final** warning.

20. She spoke with great **finality**.

Notes for Home: Your child took a pretest on pairs of words that are related to one another. *Home Activity:* Help your child learn misspelled words before the final test. Your child can underline the parts that are different in each pair and concentrate on those parts.

Spelling: Related Words

Word List

column	voice	fast	cycle	stable
columnist	vocal	fasten	bicycle	stability
face	limb	wise	human	final
facial	limber	wisdom	humane	finality

Directions: Choose the word pairs from the box in which **all** of the letters of one word are contained in the longer related word. Write each word in the correct column.

Shorter Word   **Longer Related Word**

1. _____   2. _____

3. _____   4. _____

5. _____   6. _____

7. _____   8. _____

9. _____   10. _____

11. _____   12. _____

Directions: Choose a pair of words from the box to complete each sentence. Write the words on the lines to the left.

_____ **13.** The skin on my _____ felt better after the _____ treatment.

_____ **14.**

_____ **15.** A structure won't be very _____ if its foundation lacks _____.

_____ **16.**

_____ **17.** Before I sing, I do _____ exercises to warm up my _____.

_____ **18.**

_____ **19.** It's not _____ to question the _____ of your elders.

_____ **20.**

Notes for Home: Your child spelled pairs of words that have parts that are spelled the same but pronounced differently. *Home Activity:* Say one word from the list and have your child say the related word. Then ask him or her to spell both words.